August 1

To Maria,

Be elevating
confidence.

Be On Purpose!

"Work is a source of stress and joy—we choose our focus. Few of us were taught how to build our lives and work around the desires written on our hearts. *The On-Purpose Business Person* does this by offering the insights, concepts, and methods for getting life and work in sync. Create a truly meaningful and productive future for your business or team and yourself. By reading this book, you'll discover, as I did, the joy of working smartly from your heart. You'll stress less."

Dave Zerfoss
Author, *Stress is a Choice*

"How can you be at your best in business? *The On-Purpose Business Person* is a seminal work that provides a simple, yet brilliant approach for creating the strategies, focus, and habits of health for improving your business life."

Dr. Wayne Scott Andersen
Best Selling Author *Dr. A's Habits of Health*
Co-founder of Take Shape for Life

"*The On-Purpose Business Person* is a message every business leader needs to read. I loved the story and the profound message spoken through the voice of the characters. This book holds the true essence of leadership."

Elizabeth Jeffries, CSP, CPAE,
Partner, Tweed Jeffries, LLC

"*The On-Purpose Business Person* makes perfect sense. This extraordinary book provokes deep thinking and offers hope that your life and work can definitely reflect your inner purpose."

Gary O'Malley,
O'Malley Associates

"*The On-Purpose Business Person* is a powerful paradox. It's about business, yet deeply personal. It opens a wide vista on leadership, yet sharpens a leader's focus. The message is about 'what's' and 'how's,' yet examines why they're meaningless without a compelling 'why.' It both challenges and comforts. This is a timeless book."

Bob Mueller, sales development manager,
American Suzuki Motor Corporation

"McCree is an on-purpose business. Our two-word purpose is 'realizing value' which we incorporate into everything we do. Being on-purpose has created an enjoyable workplace, a focus, and a proven profitable way of doing business."

Richard T. McCree, Jr., CEO

"Every insurance and financial advisor needs to be an on-purpose business person. Here's the way to wisely design and build your practice so both your clients and your best interests are served with performance excellence. It pays to be on-purpose."

Harry P. Hoopis, CEO
Hoopis Performance Network

"Kevin McCarthy has written an immensely valuable book for business owners and leaders who confront daily the challenge of keeping a razor sharp focus on the work that matters most to their success. It is at once practical and deep, with working strategies for finding and keeping the focus that are deeply rooted in good life principles."

Sanford Shugart, President
Valencia College

"*The On-Purpose Business Person* is one of those books that I have on my reading stack at all times. I reference it on a regular basis for issues I'm having in my company or with a business coaching client. I always trust I can find principled solutions to get things back on track in an inspiring way. This book is a must read for any business person looking to optimize their potential."

Machen MacDonald
ProBrilliance Leadership Institute

"Our vision at SOHOos.com is to establish a new global micro-economy by empowering micro-businesses and freelancers worldwide with the management tools they need to flourish. *The On-Purpose Business Person* establishes complimentary leadership thinking and strategic methods to speed collaboration and relationships toward the fulfillment of our vision."

Ron Daniels, CEO
SohoOS Ltd.

"Over my career, I've made a study of the lives of achievers who thrive on or off the job. *The On-Purpose Business Person* is a great book on how to make that happen."

Todd Duncan
Author, *High Trust Selling*

A MODERN PARABLE

The
ON-PURPOSE
Business
Person

Doing More of
What You Do Best
More Profitably

KEVIN W. McCARTHY

Published and distributed by On-Purpose Publishing
PO Box 1568 Winter Park, FL 32790
(407) 657-6000
www.on-purpose.com

For ordering information or special discounts for bulk purchases, please contact:
On-Purpose Publishing.

Cover design by Lisa Woods and Barbara Georgoudiou
Light switch design and graphics by Barbara Georgoudiou

Library of Congress Catalog Card Number: 2012943934
ISBN: 978-0-9740525-2-6

Contents

To Judith.
With this book,
Thanks Bride for your encouragement, vision, and belief in seeing
it through.
For everything else,
Thanks for putting your flag in my ship and setting sail together.

Foreword

Kevin McCarthy's first book, *The On-Purpose Person*, was a birthday present. I read the book on a business trip and was so taken by it that I called Kevin. We connected and I invited him to my offices on his next trip to California. We became instant friends and admirers of each other's work.

As a vociferous reader of books, with over 30 years of reading or browsing six to ten books per week, I've read more than 10,000 books. *The On-Purpose Person* is one of my top five favorites. Kevin's first book changes lives; *The On-Purpose Business Person* can change the world. These books deserve—no, need—to be bestsellers. Both embrace timeless messages that the world needs right here and right now.

The On-Purpose Business Person teaches you to get on-purpose, stay on-purpose, and attract the right people—all to accomplish more than you could hope and aspire to achieve alone. What could be more important?

Don't let the quick read deceive you. *The On-Purpose Business Person* has substance for the soul. This brilliant parable engages, educates, and entertains all in about the time it takes to see a movie. Few people communicate so much in so few words. Kevin shares with my departed friend, Og Mandino, the gift of presenting profound messages in memorable stories that everyone will read, re-read, share, remember, and tell again and again.

The On-Purpose Business Person works at many levels. With a quick reading, you'll end any confusion about the difference between purpose, vision, and mission statements. You'll also learn about The Four Pillars of an on-purpose business: The On-Purpose Principle, Think Inc!, The Service Model, and The Manner. There's more in this book—much, much more.

The genius of the book lies below the surface, that by using these pillars you'll excel. If you earn a paycheck, then you run a business called your career. If you own or run a business, then you know the challenges. Read this book and learn to manage your career, future, and business to become more successful than you ever dreamed.

The explosion of telecommuting, home-based businesses, and outsourcing in combination with the deepening spiritual awareness signal the desire for meaningful work as a way of life. Purpose and meaning matter. Kevin gives us a glimpse into the coming age of purpose and meaning. We have information overload and need to connect it into wisdom; this book does just that.

We may one day look back from the third millennium and see that *The On-Purpose Business Person* was the seminal work at the heart of an unmatched business revival—one that restored business as a high and noble calling of service to God, self, family, country, and our world.

With all that said, just read it! You'll love the story.

Mark Victor Hansen
Co-author, New York Times #1 bestselling
Chicken Soup for the Soul series

Preface

Do you want your life to matter and make a difference? Are you asking yourself questions like, *How do I take my life's work to the next level? How do I get better organized to be more productive? How do I help even more people? How do I fund this dream?*

Whether you acknowledge it or not, you're in business. Business isn't a dirty word. It is merely a descriptive term for the intelligent and intentional organization of work by one or more persons. The sooner you embrace this dimension to your difference-making endeavor, the more effectively and efficiently you'll realize what's pressing upon your spirit. In this context, business is a high and noble response to one's calling.

The story within these pages helps you to view your life's work through the prism of being a business person. By embracing the more strategic aspects of your vocational pursuit, you'll discover that an intelligent design and solid foundation frees you to build and create more innovatively and productively. You'll also grow, stretch, and mature into a top performing servant leader.

The Edison Example

My boyhood hero, Thomas Alva Edison is best known as the inventor of the light bulb. In their book, *The LIFE Millennium*, the editors place him first among their list of one hundred persons. Edison is often dubbed as "The Man of the Millennium." Inventing the light bulb, however, was one of his most ambitious, yet more modest achievements.

Edison was more than an inventor of products. His greater creation was the invention of the electric utility company to power those light bulbs in homes, factories, and businesses. He invented entire industries for electricity, batteries, recording, and more! Edison, the business person, founded what became General Electric Corporation. By "bringing good things to life," i.e.

commercializing his inventions into every day usefulness, he funded the scale and scope of his contribution to mankind.

Remarkably unnoticed by the public, however, Edison's greatest invention of all time is the invention of the process of inventing! His Menlo Park Laboratory in New Jersey was the world's first organized research facility. Tirelessly working, he and his team received over 400 patents. In total, he held 1,063 patents that changed the world then. Today, his many patents still brighten our lives.

Like Edison, when you gather with one or more persons around a sustainable common purpose to work toward a shared vision, you're forming an organization. Ponder the possibilities that your enterprise may meaningfully and positively ripple through the tides of lives, industry, and history. Your company of co-workers may be called a lab, agency, unit, hospital, shop, practice, school, team, shift, department, or some other term, but make no mistake about it—you're in business. Why not embrace it and excel?

Beyond good citizenship, being in business carries a duty, especially in a free society. Those of us called into the business of making a difference are charged to profit and prosper—to create a state and culture where many, not just a few, may flourish, thrive, grow, and succeed. Business people risk much to raise the standard of living of many and profits are their encore applause.

In Edison's industrial day the educational and technological base didn't support a broad entrepreneurial emancipation. In this current age of the American Dream 3.0, few such logistical barriers exist. The challenge, however, has shifted from the work of your mind and the tools in your hands to the chamber of your heart and soul. The enemies to the serving spirit are the sins of selfishness, greed, entitlement, and irresponsibility. Luke instructs, "From everyone who has been given much, much will be demanded; and from the one who has been entrusted with much, much more will be asked." Life itself is a great gift that inherently includes an activity of service called work.

We're not in Edison's day any longer, yet history offers us lessons for the future. After reading *The On-Purpose Business Person*, do an Internet search on the name Frederick W. Taylor. You'll discover that "The Old Man" earned his namesake by design. Next, consider the question, "In which age am I functioning and organizing my work?"

Light Bulbs

Within the pages of *The On-Purpose Business Person*, let's hope that you find "light bulbs" of insight as well as the light switch (Chapter 2). Apply the On-Purpose® Approach with its models, methods, and manner to design and develop a productive and cohesive organization. Discover how to lead (invent, build, and produce) the work and life that you and your associates were meant to be about individually and corporately. Let the enterprise be a tool that forges your character and compassion. In due time, joyfully share the accumulated wealth of your wisdom emerging from the blessings realized via this modern parable called *The On-Purpose Business Person*.

Right now, you face a decision: *Do I remain mired in comfortable mediocrity; or do I invest the time, effort, and intention to more fully answer the vocational call upon my life by putting my purpose into play by design?* Choose the latter and you, too, will be an on-purpose business person in creation. Read on!

Be On-Purpose!
Kevin W. McCarthy

Acknowledgments

Fortunately for me, I'm blessed with an engaged and supportive cast through the years. Julie Holzmann has provided regular proofreading, copyediting, prompting, and suggestions to my creative works for over a decade. Coming alongside me administratively have been Sue Coleman, Nicole Sankovic, Diana Walker, and Cheryl Foca. Barbara Georgoudiou brings her creative brilliance to the graphics and On-Purpose® branding. My business partners, Mary Tomlinson in the United States, and Edward and Angela Gifford in Australia, have all contributed with me to bring these concepts to life in client organizations.

Clients must be thanked, also. Entrusting their core business strategy and design to us as their business advisors is a role we take seriously. Performance matters in the marketplace and we're proud to have had a hand at the foundations of the development, growth, and results for these leaders and team members. Client success is our success and further validation of the importance and power found being in the business of being on-purpose.

(In the back section, please see the Acknowledgments for the original 1998 edition that was titled, *The On-Purpose Business*.)

1
The Interview

▼

There are two fundamentally differing views of human nature and work. The "objective view" sees work as a source of economic means. The "subjective view" is concerned with the effects of work on the person. By the early twenty-first century, quality will become a commodity, and companies will be distinguished by the wholeness of their people.

Bill O'Brien
former CEO,
Hanover Insurance Company

"She's here," chirped Jackie, the man's assistant. "The receptionist just called. I'll greet her, okay?"

"Please. Let me gather my thoughts before the interview," responded the man.

"She" was a reporter from *The Wall Street Journal.* Two years ago an article in this newspaper had forecast the imminent demise of the company. Her arrival today signaled a broad recognition of a corporate renewal nothing less than spectacular.

Anticipating her typical questions about his "secrets" on the turnaround, he could only smile to himself and wonder, *How do I tell her a gold pocket watch made all the difference?* Picking up the timepiece from its desk stand, he caressed it in his left palm and then wound it. The extraordinary workmanship, beauty, and jeweled mechanism made it an object of functional art. Neither its art nor its function made it valuable. This watch has a story.

Opening the delicate gold locket cover and thumbing the inscription, he read, "To Frederick W. Taylor, in honor of forty-eight years of faithful service and leadership." He smiled in fond remembrance of his departed boss and influencer.

This watch served as a tangible remembrance of a man, his era, and lifestyle; it was a symbol of the past, a reminder in the present, and a touchstone for the future. The ever-ticking watch reminded him of lessons learned in business and, importantly, in life.

His mind flashed to Fred Taylor's retirement party two years earlier...

▼ ▼ ▼

The Old Man's Watch

Fred's nickname was "The Old Man." His career had begun as a teenager in the mailroom and ended over four decades later while serving as the chief executive officer. Despite Fred's shortcomings, the man had to admire his lifetime accomplishments. With a firm hand at the helm, Fred Taylor was the company and the company was Fred.

Still, the man couldn't help thinking *It's a good thing The Old Man's retiring*. A recent heart attack provided a graceful early exit. Undoubtedly, a healthy Fred would have been pressured by the board of directors to step aside. As Fred told it, he was "going out on top — a winner," but in almost everyone else's mind, The Old Man was self-deceived. The company was dangerously past due for a competitive overhaul — beginning at the top.

Business had changed, as had the times, and The Old Man fought it hard. Navigating the shifting currents of the economy and the ever-quickening rapids of business overwhelmed Fred. "Gone are the good old days," he would lament. Clinging to old patterns and perspectives, Fred's methods were no longer relevant. He called it "sticking to fundamentals," except that the fundamentals had changed.

Years ago, under Fred's command, the company had fallen into a comfort zone, a subtle winner's arrogance. As the executives grew more content and self-satisfied, competitors emerged. It was unimaginable that small start-ups could touch, let alone erode, the market leadership of the company.

Now they struggled just to keep up. The man thought, *We're like a champion prizefighter who stayed in the ring one too many bouts.* Momentum and reputation sustained the business and masked many problems. The ultimate undoing of the business wasn't going to be competition — it would be denial.

The stakes were high and the margin for error thin. Rising expenses and falling prices were squeezing profits. Cash was tight. Longtime customers were moving to smaller, faster, lower-priced producers. The priorities of the company and the employees were often at cross-purposes. Turf battles between vice presidents were the norm.

Product quality was suffering. It was a wonder that product got out the door; and when it did ship, defects or shipping mistakes were creating frequent and costly returns and remakes. The competitive edge was blunt, and customer complaints soared. Even their largest and best contract customer, the GEOMay Company, lodged complaint after complaint.

Fred hadn't grasped the threat to the very existence of the business. Leading from the past, he ruled with a stubborn, tightfisted hold. A polite mutiny stirred. The vice presidents reported what he wanted to hear but did as they saw fit to be in the best interests of the company, but mostly themselves. Their intentions were positive, but their results were not. "White lies" hamstrung the operation and divided the executives and their minions. The trickle of deceit became a stream of ethical compromises where truth was just an inconvenience.

Fred's gold pocket watch symbolized the best of a bygone era that revered truth and values — a time when one's character and reputation clearly stood above the current quarterly earnings and personal fortune, a time when one's life was more than a job and collective status symbols.

The man knew a gold retirement watch was unlikely to be in his future. The global nature of business; the reach of technology, mergers, and changes in distribution; the Internet; and the swings in consumer demands were a few of the factors bursting the once-secure career with a single company.

Fred began his farewell address, "Forty-eight years ago this past June, I joined this company...." The man's thoughts drifted from The Old Man's retirement rhapsody to the enormous challenges that lay before him as Fred's replacement. To calm the whirlwind of confusing thoughts and emotions blowing through his mind, he needed help.

He knew just the person to call: his old friend, the Professor....

▼ ▼ ▼

The Man's Story

Jackie escorted the reporter into the man's office. After a few pleasantries, the interview began. "To what do you attribute the successful turnaround of this company?" she asked right on cue.

Holding the timepiece in his hand, the man began, "Do you see this gold pocket watch?"

2
Purpose Is at the Heart

▼

Effective leaders delegate a good many things; they have to or they drown in trivia. They do not delegate the one thing that only they can do with excellence, the one thing that will make a difference, the one thing that will set the standards, the one thing they want to be remembered for. They do it.

Peter F. Drucker
The Leader of the Future

Leaning back in his chair, the Professor sat staring out his office window. Unnoticed, the man entered the office and jested, "Caught you! Daydreaming again."

Twirling to face the man, the Professor laughed, stood, and threw open his arms. The friends embraced. "I was on a two-minute vacation. It's a relaxation technique a professor colleague taught me. He's compiled *Dr. Brophy's Guidebook of Two-Minute Vacations* that's filled with short games, getaways, and ideas to recreate. You caught me being on-purpose."

"As always," the man laughed.

Closing his door for privacy, the Professor resumed, "So what's the purpose of your visit?"

The man and the Professor had a trusted history, so the man immediately disclosed, "Briefly ... I'm the new president of my company. It's in shambles, and ... I need help, now!"

"What's at stake?" asked the Professor.

Pondering the question for a moment, the man answered, "The future of the company and the jobs of many people, including mine."

"Hm-m-m," the Professor sighed as he scratched behind his right ear. "Step one, what's the purpose of your organization?"

The man replied, "We have a mission statement."

Wincing, the Professor asked, "What's it say?"

The man stammered with embarrassment, "Huh? I, er, ah — I don't know."

The Professor shook his head in disbelief. "Amazing! The president of the company doesn't know the *mission statement!* Call your office and have it sent to your phone." The Professor's eyes narrowed. "And it's a *purpose statement* not a mission statement. Get it right!"

"Pardon my mix-up," the man said, feeling the Professor's heat. He sent a text to Jackie requesting it.

The Professor didn't buy the apology. "It's no mix-up. It's a lack of basic understanding of the principles of being on-purpose. Don't casually swap purpose, vision, and mission. They're not synonyms. The misuse of these rich words has significance to the very essence of life itself."

His curiosity piqued, the man asked, "Professor, remind me, what *is* the difference between purpose, vision, and mission? Obviously, I still don't get it."

In a measured voice and with a big grin, the Professor announced, "I will joyfully explain the difference. I *love* to clarify that question. First, there is only one purpose. But there are many visions — and several missions for each vision."

The man jotted notes in a journal.

The Professor continued, "Next, we'll reference purpose, vision, mission, plus values to your body."

"To my body?" inquired the man.

"Yes! Their meaning is more visceral this way. You need an On-Purpose Pal to help you remember.

"First, purpose is from the heart. Draw a big, broad heart in the middle of your paper and label it 'Purpose.'" The man did as

instructed.

"Purpose resides in the heart," the Professor said. "The ancient Greeks said the heart is where mind, body, and soul converge. I agree. Purpose envelops love. So be in touch with your heart," he said while lightly drumming with his hand at the center of his chest to indicate his heart.

The Professor continued their lesson. "Next is vision. Above the heart, draw a circle for a head. Let's put a face on our pal by adding two bright eyes and a big smile. Label the head 'Vision.'"

"Vision resides in your mind's eye. It is your dreams and possibilities.

"Close your eyes." The man did as he was told. "Now imagine a blue elephant... its tusks are green... and its toenails are painted hot pink... and it's wearing purple boxer shorts with yellow polka dots. Do you see it?"

The man burst into laughter. "What a sight!"

"That's your mind's eye. Images power the imagination. Now, with your eyes still closed, see your business in its ultimate vision or form. Dream in rich detail." While pacing meditatively, the Professor engaged the man's imagination. "Who are your customers and why? How are they served? What plans, people, and processes are in place to ensure successful customer experiences? How does it feel walking around your business?

"See your annual report. What do the sales and profit charts look like?

"Think about the people working there — are they smiling, happy... enthusiastic, confident... excited and purposeful?

"Are you good corporate citizens?

"What engages your heart, head, and hands on a day-to-day basis? On what basis are you making decisions?"

The man sat with eyes closed and a smile from ear to ear. Finally he said, "This is terrific."

"And it all resides where?"

"In my imagination, or my mind's eye as you describe it," the man answered.

"Yes. Your purpose and vision need to be connected and aligned. A vision not anchored in your purpose is most often just a costly distraction."

The man opened his eyes and jotted a couple more notes. "You're right about vision without purpose," he said. "I've chased some dreams only to find they weren't meaningful." He prompted the Professor. "Tell me about missions."

"Let's put some hands and feet on your On-Purpose Pal."

The Professor continued, "Missions are what we do to fulfill the vision that is anchored in our purpose. Missions are the 'doing' aspects of our lives. Purpose is the being, and visions are the seeing."

"For the first time," the man noted, "the subtle difference in these words is making sense. They're not synonyms!" Pressing the Professor, he asked, "Where are our values reflected on the body?"

"Where do you think?" countered the Professor.

"The heart?" the man guessed.

"Well, we already said the heart is our purpose. Want a clue?" he offered. The man nodded compliantly. "If you violate your values, where will you feel it?"

The man remarked, "In my gut. You know, the expression 'My gut tells me something's not right about this.' Correct?"

"Yes, your gut! The other place for values is your throat. It's the gatekeeper to outer temptations. In other words, if a vendor attempts an illegal kickback in exchange for a contract, you would have a choking or a gag response. Your values are warning you not to mistakenly ingest their indecent proposal. Otherwise, you would live with that compromise in your gut. Violate your values frequently, and it's called an ulcer.

"Back to drawing. Put a small circle at the throat and a big oval at the belly to symbolize values on your body."

"I like it," the man said. "I won't forget my on-purpose pal."

The Professor posed the question, "What's the worst violation of one's values?"

"Being off-purpose?" the man guessed.

"Yes! Being off-purpose is the ultimate separation and loss of integrity. It leaves us with an empty and disintegrated feeling. When we're off-purpose, we'll more easily crave artificial fulfillment instead of the pure nourishment of purpose. People indulge in drugs and alcohol, food, chocolate, sex, work, shame, or other destructive behaviors. When hopelessness gains a foothold, it is an unyielding master."

The man winced. "Wow! I've been known to indulge. That's an intense list and an even more worrisome outcome."

"Align your purpose, visions, and missions. Another way of saying it is, when we've aligned our heart, head, and hands with our values, then, we're living with integrity. That's being on-purpose.

"Let's look at our friend the On-Purpose Pal. It isn't enough to know your purpose, vision, missions, and values. They must all be connected, aligned, and coordinated. So let's join the parts so your heart, head, hands and feet, and values are fully aligned and integrated."

The Professor continued, "As the leader of the company, your integrity is the company standard. If you want the business to be on-purpose, you must be an on-purpose leader.

"By the way, everyone is a leader. Whether you're the company president or a mailroom clerk, you bring your purpose to the position. The scale and scope of authority is different for each of us."

The Professor glanced at his watch. "I have a class in fifteen minutes. I need to run shortly, so let's overview and review each strategic element within the On-Purpose Pal. Pardon the lecture, but take notes.

"Purpose builds on our past, lives in our present, and holds hope for our future. A purpose statement preamble begins with 'I exist to serve by....' Therefore, purpose is the ultimate service concept.

"Now, consider your customer service programs and hiring in light of purpose. Purpose is spiritual DNA from which our vision and missions emerge. Purpose is God's will for your life. Purpose is infinite and eternal."

The man's eyes opened widely.

"Purpose is spiritual electricity," the Professor continued. "Like electricity, it has been around since the beginning of time. But only after Benjamin Franklin identified and named electricity did people harness its awesome power. Edison's light bulb, Bell's telephone, the computer, television, smartphone, and all the other electronic devices emerged thanks to a man, a kite, and a key.

"We're in our infancy when it comes to understanding and harnessing the power of purpose. Imagine the possibilities in our lives and society as our understanding and use of purpose mature. This, you may recall," the Professor said as he pointed to a poster with a light switch, "is the symbol of the on-purpose person. It reminds us to stay connected with our higher power and to turn it on."

"I like the analogy," the man commented. "Go on, please."

"Vision answers the question, 'Where are we going?' It is our hope; it inspires us today. It resides in our mind's eye or imagination. Vision is a developing snapshot of our future. Vision is blue-sky thinking and dreaming crystallized into words and images that capture our heart. We can have an overall vision for our life plus visions for each area of life—financial, vocational, social, family, physical, mental, and spiritual.

"Missions are our doings in the present, right now, today. They are the current means and actions at hand. Missions focus on outward actions and address the question, 'What do we need to be doing today to fulfill and express our purpose and advance us toward our vision?' Missions are measurable, finite, and composed of specific goals with definite beginnings and endings.

"Values are learned and revealed internal governors of right and wrong that we feel in our gut and throat. Values are timeless regulators of our purpose in the world about us. They help us choose what is most important."

An email alert sounded on the man's phone. Checking it, the man saw that the company mission statement had arrived. From the Professor's printer he printed two copies.

3
The Purpose Statement

▼

My job is in line with the president's job—to keep people happy.

John Wiggins
1995 Ruffies Trash Bags
National Sanitation Worker of the Year

The Professor read it aloud: "Our mission is to pursue excellence by profitably serving our customers and adding value through quality products and services as the national leader in our industry while delivering a high rate of return to our stockholders."

The man was embarrassed. "That's the ultimate blah mission statement," he blurted. "It sounds like we bought a book of catchy business phrases and combined a bunch of 'em. Nine months of meetings and tens of thousands of dollars to write that! It lacks personality, punch, and heart."

The Professor burst into laughter. "Well said! No wonder you couldn't remember it. Wad it into a ball and trash it."

The man obeyed. Then he asked, "What do I do next?"

"Turning around the company starts with a purpose statement and alignment with it. It influences your plan, people, process, and performance for your customers, shareholders, and community."

"You're right. It's no wonder we're adrift. Professor, tell me more about a purpose statement."

The Professor explained, "A purpose statement is simply two power-packed words honed in on the very uniqueness of the person or organization. It answers the question, 'Why do I exist?' The preamble begins with 'I exist to serve by...' and ends with two words."

"Two words—that's it?" the man asked.

"That's it. Purpose is like spiritual DNA. Think of the two words as the X and Y chromosomes of the soul. Here are actual examples of purpose statements: I exist to serve by... *Setting Free*; *Awakening Worth*; *Celebrating Nature*; *Igniting Dignity*; *Inspiring Insight*; and *Liberating Greatness*. From these seeds individuals and organizations have grown and prospered, on-purpose!"

The man observed, "All the X chromosome words end with -*ing*, don't they?"

"Yes. That shows the forever nature of being on-purpose. Remember, our purpose lives in our past, present, and future into eternity. It isn't a defining event; it's a state of being."

"What about the second word, Professor? What's its role?"

"The second half of the purpose statement is the object of the activity. It brings clarity and depth."

The man started to stand up. "Professor, I know you have class shortly. I've got it. Thanks! How will I ever repay you?"

"Not so fast with the adieu," said the Professor. "You came here because your business is in shambles, remember?"

"That's right."

The Professor looked the man dead in the eyes and said, "You need help. A purpose statement is a starting point, not a finish line. What you want is an on-purpose business. You need a business person to help you. Let me reacquaint you with..."

"Bob Scott!" exclaimed the man as he tapped his forehead. The Professor nodded his agreement. "Why didn't I think of him before? Back when I first met Bob, I told him I noticed he had a high-performance team at his company.

"Bob said, 'Thank you. We're an on-purpose business.'

"I asked, 'What do you mean by that, Bob?'

"'We're very clear about the purpose of our company. We encourage each person to become an on-purpose person. We can't change people; we do want them to become increasingly more aware of who they are and what's important to them. Those insights are the beginning of true personal leadership. It's a powerful and fulfilling linkage when the purpose of the person is aligned with the purpose of the organization.'

"Professor, some time ago I asked Bob how to develop an on-purpose business. At the time, he waved me off and said, 'Let's hold that conversation until another day.' In so many words he said my first priority was personal clarity around my purpose, and after that, we could address the needs of my organization."

"Now you are ready," encouraged the Professor.

The Professor and the man gave each other a hug. Then the Professor went off to his class, while the man headed to his car to call Bob Scott and arrange a meeting.

4

The Age of Purpose

▼

When our first parents were driven out of Paradise, Adam remarked to Eve, "My dear, we live in an age of transition."

W. R. Inge (1860–1954)
Dean, St. Paul's Church, London

Resting comfortably in a large upholstered chair, the man soaked in the ambience of Bob Scott's office. The warm setting of traditional furnishings and hardwood floors covered with oriental rugs reflected the person. Hunter green walls held magnificent oil paintings, charcoals, and etchings of presidents and landscapes. Contrasting this motif was a gleaming bank of computers on Bob's desk.

They chatted until the man directed the conversation. "Please tell me about creating an on-purpose business."

"Let's get started," agreed Bob. "We'll begin with the three perspectives. The first is our place in the stream of history. The second is the organization relative to society. And the third is the interplay of the person, the business, and the society. These three perspectives are the backdrop of clues and patterns that help us anticipate the path ahead."

"So we can plan accordingly?" asked the man.

"Yes," Bob said. "First, let's look at our place in an abbreviated history of the world. We live in the Knowledge Age, which advanced from the Industrial Age, which grew from the Agricultural Age, which was produced from the Stone Age. Right?"

"Right," agreed the man.

"What is the age beyond this present age?"

"I'm having enough trouble figuring out this present age," quipped the man. "What's the answer?"

"Not so fast," said Bob coyly. "Think this through. Here's a hint. Look at the relationship of technology and work. Through the ages we've risen from being hunters and gatherers to farmers to industrial workers to knowledge workers. How has the nature of our day-to-day work changed?"

The man's eyes lit up. "We've shifted from the work of our hands to the work of our heads."

"And what's the next logical progression?" prodded Bob.

The man deliberated further. Suddenly, he snapped his fingers in realization. "It's like the On-Purpose Pal in reverse! We're going from our hands to our heads to our hearts."

"Right," Bob affirmed. "Paradoxically, in the midst of a seemingly chaotic and meaningless world, our society is speeding to the Age of Purpose. As our knowledge grows, we realize even more of what we don't understand. More knowledge will never be the answer. Meaning in life is an inner quality of which the mind is but a conduit."

"So how do I apply this perspective today?"

Bob answered, "Perspective number two is an organizational perspective. The way to the right answers is to ask the right questions:

- How might your company operate in the coming Age of Purpose?
- What are the advantages of this insight?
- How can extraordinary people be attracted to work in this future age?
- What will be the nature of business?
- Will work support the family or the family support work?
- Can work become a place where the average person makes a positive difference in society?

"On-Purpose offers solutions to these questions," Bob continued. "The bottom line is that forward-thinking organizations offering meaningful opportunity to attract employees and engage customers will hold a strategic advantage over those that don't."

"I need it now," the man confessed.

"No, you don't," Bob corrected. "This is a strategic advantage, but that's missing the mark. This isn't about competition, per se. It is about the collaboration of people and organizations doing more of what they do best more profitably."

"This is different," the man remarked. "And the third perspective is...?"

"Your personal perspective is the most important because you control it. Your viewpoint is your rudder to navigate the shifting currents of society and business.

"Along this line," Bob challenged, "why did you wait so long to come see me about being on-purpose in business?"

"I was appointed president by the board only a few months ago. With Fred Taylor still there, the transfer of responsibility didn't come until recently."

Bob pressed, "I'll rephrase the question. Why did you wait until you became president? You needed to be in the On-Purpose Process long before now."

"It wasn't as critical as it is now," said the man, cringing even as the words left his mouth.

"Excuses," Bob declared. "Responsibility follows preparedness. Are you *really* prepared to lead or do you just hold the office of President and CEO?"

Bull's-eye! What a startling realization. Inside a few minutes Bob had nailed the man's darkest doubt. Was he adequately prepared to fulfill his long-held dream of leading the company? Was he a leader?

Thankfully, Bob was here to help him not hammer him. "You're right," the man admitted. "It's scary being responsible for a business. This is virgin territory for me. I need your help because I lack... a president's perspective and experience."

Bob comforted him by saying, "On-Purpose yields perspective but not experience. Experience you'll need to gain on your own."

The man asked, "Does anyone understand this brave new world of technology and change?"

"Yes, but their understanding isn't like what you're thinking. I'm talking about the business of business — what it means to run an organization, large or small. There are universal patterns to designing and building an organization. Learn these, use these, and you'll have very high organizational intelligence."

"What patterns?" queried the man.

"They're the Four Pillars of an on-purpose business. They'll help you align and integrate the heart, head, and hands in more profitable service."

"It sounds too simple," the man remarked.

"On the first day of our new employee orientation we introduce the Four Pillars. Executives, department heads, mailroom clerks, receptionists, salespeople — everyone knows and uses them. By sharing a common method the business of doing business becomes less complicated and more productive. I like that because it is good for the team and profitable for the company."

"You're committed to this, aren't you?" the man observed.

"Totally," Bob declared. "Being an on-purpose business person will transform your leadership and therefore your business. The members of your team will see the company, their jobs, and their lives from that of being the president of their own business. Your team members will rise to new heights of fun, performance, and reward."

"Can something this simple be that potent?"

"Don't make that mistake. Is complexity in working together somehow a strategic advantage?"

"I guess not," conceded the man.

"I have another question for you, Bob. Why? Why are you helping me learn this?"

Bob laughed. "I'm helping me...you...and this community. This is the cooperation I spoke of earlier. Sharing this is on-purpose for me. I'm honored and privileged to do it.

"But there's one condition," Bob added. "Promise me that when the time is right, you'll do the same for another person. As I am your on-purpose pal now, will you freely share the Four Pillars in the future with another?"

The man nodded and said "Agreed! That's assuming I like it."

"That's fair," Bob said. "Let's toast this occasion with a coffee from The Club." They rose from their chairs and walked to The Club, a restaurant adjoining the R. D. Scott Company offices. "I'll give you an overview of the Four Pillars."

5
The Four Pillars

▼

This company has the brain
of a for-profit and the soul
of a not-for-profit.

Rebecca Maddox
Inc. Your Dreams

A friendly hostess at The Club seated Bob and the man at a window overlooking the tranquil downtown park. A waiter promptly greeted them.

"Good morning, gentlemen. Hi, Bob!" He then turned to the man. "Welcome to The Club, sir."

"Good morning, Dave," Bob returned. "I'll have a coffee, black, please."

"Same for me," said the man.

"Right away, gentlemen." Dave headed to the kitchen.

Bob Scott explained, "Each of the Four Pillars is associated with a word beginning with the letter *M*. They are the Meaning, Mindset, Method, and Manner, respectively.

"Here's a quick overview." Borrowing the man's journal he numbered and labeled each corner of the page, 1, 2, 3, and 4.

With his pen point resting in the upper left corner, he began, "Pillar One: The Meaning is the heart of it, or the On-Purpose Principle. This describes the purpose of the person aligning with the purpose of the organization. We'll discuss Pillar One in a little bit."

Moving the pen to the upper right corner, Bob explained, "Pillar Two is the Mindset: *Think Inc!* This is an abbreviation for Think Incorporated. It means we need to be, think, and act as the president of our own company. The exclamation point creates an encouraging affirmation. I'm 'Bob, Inc!' Your assistant is 'Jackie, Inc!' Understand?"

"Yes," said the man. Rubbing his chin, he admitted, "I haven't been doing *Think Inc!*"

"It's a learned choice." Bob added, "Each of us *is* a business of one. Commissioned salespeople and small business owners are acutely aware of this reality. Yet, the concept applies equally well to salaried and hourly people. They simply contract their services with one customer—their employer. Entrepreneurs and business owners epitomize the concept, but it isn't theirs exclusively.

"Instilling and supporting the *Think Inc!* mindset regardless of our position, experience, or compensation is a profound mental shift. Most people aren't used to thinking as though they have a profit-and-loss responsibility. High personal responsibility and consequences are part of the deal.

"You'll soon meet Frances Attwood, a real estate broker, former team member, and friend. She'll share her story of *Think Inc!*"

The man gravitated to *Think Inc!* This was the mindset he felt was dulled reporting to Fred Taylor and was dormant in his team and company. They lacked an entrepreneurial edge.

"Pillar Three is the Service Model, the method for designing and building any organization," Bob resumed, indicating the lower left corner of the paper. "Through Hal Trudy, my mentor and first on-purpose partner, you will be ... shall we say, cultivated for your new role. Hal led a highly successful and profitable company prior to his retirement. The people in Hal's company learned and applied the Four Pillars. His business was highly valued because of the quality of its people. They're TOP Performers. By the way," Bob said, "TOP is an acronym for 'The On-Purpose.' Therefore, 'TOP Performer' means The On-Purpose Performer—that's also the name of our employee orientation.

"Hal Trudy is an extraordinary man who retired from his business a wealthy man in many ways. The transition for the next CEO was seamless — in contrast to your transition."

"I definitely look forward to meeting him," remarked the man. "Now, what about Pillar Four?"

In a measured voice Bob revealed, "Pillar Four: The Manner is about conducting one's business. That is a profound statement whether you realize it or not. This is why I urge you to take a paced approach to redeveloping your company. Business is a marathon, not a sprint. Altering the culture in your organization takes time rather than one swift pass of a laser-printed edict. It's one person, one heart, one head, and one pair of hands at a time."

The man asked, "Okay, what's the Manner?"

"The Manner is," Bob stated, "doing more of what you do best more profitably."

"Doing more of...what I do best...more profitably," the man repeated softly and slowly. "Doing more of...what I do best...more profitably." Rolling the words in his mind, he finally snapped his fingers in appreciation. "Yes, I would love to do more of what I do best more profitably. That would be fun!"

Now briefed on the Four Pillars, the man immediately began trying to make sense of it. "So building an on-purpose business is a matter of understanding and using the Four Pillars?"

"One closing comment," Bob inserted. "This begins with you. Be patient with the business for a time. You have to become a product of the Pillars yourself. As you master them, then you can begin to share and leverage them throughout your team."

"So an on-purpose business is really a community," assessed the man, "with a common means of interacting and organizing. Fewer structural issues get in the way of progress and business."

"Exactly," acknowledged Bob.

"Wow!" exclaimed the man. "It never dawned on me that our greatest challenges may be in how our business is organized. Let's get started on Pillar One."

6
Pillar One:
The On-Purpose Principle

▼

Step One: Establish constancy of purpose at the macro and micro level with the focus on the customer.

W. Edwards Deming
"Fourteen Steps to Quality"

"Pillar One: the Meaning embodies the On-Purpose Principle," Bob Scott began. "It is represented with the following diagram." Bob began drawing in the man's journal.

The On-Purpose Principle™

He explained, "This equation reads as 'The purpose of the person (Pp) aligned with the purpose of the organization (Po).' The On-Purpose Principle depicts the presence and alignment of two states: significance and belonging. These are two powerful needs people have. High alignment results in feelings of meaningful contribution. In other words, being on-purpose.

"Like Einstein's theory of relativity, $E=mc^2$, this depiction distills several complex concepts into something elegantly useful.

"The On-Purpose Principle is the only meaningful linkage between a person and an organization. A person and the legal entity, called a business in your case, have no natural affinity except a common purpose—the bond of the collective spirit of its people. A paycheck without purpose is just a mercenary's fee — an empty exchange for a task."

The man countered, "My boss, Fred Taylor, used to say, 'You need to separate your personal life from your business life.' This runs counter to conventional wisdom."

"Yes, it does," Bob unapologetically answered. "That Industrial Age mentality is as obsolete as the typewriter. A harsh separation of one's business and personal life isn't effective anymore. Our vocation can be a meaningful and integrated expression of our purpose. We need to be whole."

The man brushed the last remark aside with "That's idealistic."

"So, what's your ideal instead?" countered Bob.

"Work is work, and that's the way it is."

"That's not an ideal. That's a resignation to mindless mediocrity and a rationale for heartlessness."

Resting his head on his right hand, the man conceded. "Perhaps you're right. Please, go on."

Bob continued, "Work as an expression of your purpose will become apparent in due course. Find opportunities that you can believe in with your heart, and you'll prosper. Ignore the On-Purpose Principle and you're ultimately an empty suit, conforming to ever-tightening systems and structures attempting to induce and manipulate you into desired behaviors and results.

"Motivation is from within. Tap it within yourself and you'll know how to help others do the same. Everyone wins."

"That's very high alignment," the man commented.

"Exactly," Bob answered and then added, "low-alignment people are easy to spot. They stay unhappy in jobs for years or even longer until retirement just for the paycheck. They don't understand that life is too precious to sell out for a few dollars.

"The subtle yet costly killer of morale, quality, and profits is low alignment. Low-alignment people are often labeled as having a bad attitude. In fact, their lives and situations are often overrun with fear spiced with the lack of confidence, worth, and faith."

The man nodded his head in total agreement. Bob pressed on. "Now imagine someone who believes life is meaningless. Alignment isn't possible because he or she brings no sense of a purpose into the relationship. Look for men and women seeking to make a difference with their lives. They care about something. In the final analysis, one's heart"—Bob placed his fist over his heart— "has to be in anything to excel — a marriage, a job, a relationship, anything. Love matters in life and work."

The man picked up on the comment. "I see high alignment by the way a person's eyes light up, or by his or her body language and energy."

"Yes, yes," Bob agreed. "Imagine a workplace where people have the glint of purpose in their eyes and a bounce in their step. Purpose matters because it is a matter of the heart. I can't say that enough." Bob repeatedly tapped at the On-Purpose Principle in the man's journal to make his point. "This pillar is the heart and soul of an on-purpose business."

"When I walk into your business, I sense that," the man observed.

"Thank you! That's a high compliment."

Then Bob pressed on. "Have you ever heard someone say, 'I want to make a difference' or 'I want to know that my life matters'?"

"Sure, all the time."

"That's an inborn desire for the On-Purpose Principle. That is the leadership spark."

"Yes! That makes total sense," exclaimed the man. "As leaders we have an enormous responsibility to articulate and demonstrate the purpose of the organization. Right?"

"Absolutely. Articulating and communicating the purpose of the organization is pivotal to anyone's performance, but especially us as chief executive officers. In our roles, we characterize the corporate culture. A clear and succinctly stated purpose attracts and helps to retain team members who fit."

The man agreed. "Persons with their heart in their work connect with the work, care that it's right, and are more apt to self-manage better. They're the best quality control available. It's not policies, per se. An authentic desire to contribute rightly and responsibly to the best of their ability results from having a powerful reason or 'a why' for what they're doing. They have a 'good attitude.'"

With a sudden shift in countenance, the man covered his eyes with his right hand and began a troubled massage of his temples with his thumb and index finger. "I just realized something," he moaned. "Without a strong 'organizational why,' everyone creates his or her own 'why.' All those well-intended 'whys' ultimately come to cross-purposes and cause utter chaos. That's my company."

"This," Bob said as he pointed with his pen repeatedly to the drawing of the On-Purpose Principle, "is the most powerful concept and tool you'll ever learn about leading people and fashioning a sustainable, healthy, and service-hearted organization. Pillar One is a must if your business is to be a TOP Performer, period."

The man's eyes lit up. "I see it. Now how do I use it?"

Bob laughed. "Great question! You'll use it everywhere and all the time, but it is subtle. You'll use the On-Purpose Principle when you hire; when you target customer segments; when you engage a vendor; when you do strategic planning; when you develop a new program, such as a marketing or sales program; even in your accounting and information systems. When you forge a strategic alliance or merger, you'll be looking at your potential partner in terms of alignment. You'll use it in your day-to-day activities such as writing a letter, making a phone call, or scheduling your appointments. With this insight it becomes obvious and inescapable, a second nature."

"Bob, please help me make this come alive in my business," the man said.

"No problem." Bob smiled. "You need to know about The On-Purpose Quadrant."

7

TOP Performer

▼

To have a path of knowledge, a path with a heart, makes for a
joyful journey…and is the only conceivable way to live. We must
then think carefully about our paths before we set out on them, for
by the time a person discovers that his path "has no heart," the
path is ready to kill him. At that point few of us have the courage
to abandon the path, lethal as it may be, because we have invested
so much in it, and to choose a new path seems so dangerous, even
irresponsible. And so we continue dutifully, if joylessly, along.

Carlos Castaneda
The Fire from Within

Bob flipped to a new page in the man's journal. He drew a large
rectangle and divided it into four boxes so it resembled a window
with four panes. "The On-Purpose Quadrant illustrates the
relationship of two alignments." Holding up two fingers on his
right hand, he began, "The two types of alignment are Technical
and Tingle."

Outside and down the left side of the window he wrote
TECHNICAL. "Technical is the knowledge, experience, and talent
needed to do a job, process, or business. It's the ability to get the
job done."

"What in the world is Tingle?" prompted the man.

Writing *TINGLE* at the outside bottom and center of the
window, Bob continued, "Tingle is a … well … a feeling, an inner
desire to excel, to achieve high satisfaction. Tingle is the love of the
work. High tingle is when you're head over heels in love; you're
having the time of your life with goose bumps of excitement. You

feel great about what you're doing, where you're headed, and who you are."

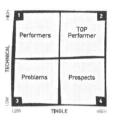

"Tingle!" The man chuckled as he said, "You and the Professor keep things so real, so ... user-friendly."

"C'mon, life's tough enough," Bob offered. "Why mess it up with unneeded complexity? Have some fun. Tingle does describe the feeling."

"You're right," the man conceded. "I never thought of Tingle in my work. Maybe that's my problem, I don't expect any Tingle."

Bob elaborated. "High-Tingle people use words to describe their work like: calling, committed, fit, engaged, gifted, and passion. We talk in terms of coming from the heart. We're positive, hope-filled people."

Bob pointed back to the journal. "This model integrates Technical and Tingle so we can apply the On-Purpose Principle. Think of it as a window on people at work." He filled in each quadrant or windowpane. Now pointing with his pen to the model, Bob posed, "If you want to hire or promote the best possible people, from which quadrant will you select your candidates?"

"No doubt, Quadrant 2—high Technical and high Tingle."

"Why?" Bob asked.

"They're the High-Technical and High-Tingle people—the complete package. They're fully on board with the purpose of the organization and doing the work in a highly satisfactory manner."

"Exactly," Bob agreed. "You'll see new hires and promotions with fresh insight thanks to TOP Quadrant. Whenever you hear 'TOP Performer,' think of a person with High-Technical *and* High-Tingle alignment. High Performers, found in quadrant 1, are markedly different from TOP Performers in Quadrant 2.

"TOP Performers are the best people to hire and promote, period. Avoid Problems. Relentlessly search for TOP Performers and cultivate Prospects.

"Most of us inadvertently bias our hiring toward high Performers because Technical is the more obvious need and easier to assess. Alone, however, it's an insufficient benchmark, more from ignorance than intention."

The man sat thinking, *This is so apparent. Yet, until now, I'd never thought or heard of it. "Tingle" puts into a word the feeling I have when I walk into the R. D. Scott Company. It's a High-Tingle workplace — an entirely different dimension, attitude, and culture is at work. It is a sense of significance, belonging, and contribution.*

Bob sensed the man's contemplative manner and asked, "Are the lights on in there?"

"My light switch is definitely turned on. This makes so much sense. We lack Tingle in my business," the man confided. "We are clueless. For this 'window on work,' what insight might you offer for the other panes?"

Bob said, "Panes 2 and 3 are obvious. Quad 2, or TOP Performer, as we discussed, depicts the ideal candidates with High Technical and High Tingle. The Problems in Quad 3 have low capacity to perform the job and little heart for it. These candidates are a poor fit, period, and probably need to have their future freed up to work elsewhere."

Chuckling, the man interpreted, "Pains are in pane 3. 'Free up' their future means to fire them, right?"

"Not exactly," Bob corrected, "We only fire for clear cause. We acknowledge our role and responsibility in a poor hiring fit. The former team member is provided outplacement services to help them find a Prospect or TOP Performer position elsewhere."

"That's nice of you. We just terminate them," the man informed, "so we can cut our losses."

"But," Bob countered, "you don't cut your losses; you risk increasing them. Treating people irresponsibly or disrespectfully always comes back to haunt you directly or indirectly. A firm, yet dignified departure, has a higher probability of a good long-term outcome for all. Treat a Problem as you would like one of your disgruntled customers to treat you."

"Whoa! That *is* different! I get it," the man acknowledged.

Windows of Insight

"Great! Quads 1 and 4 are not so apparent. To explain these," Bob warned, "I'll use extreme lows and highs to make the point. But the fact is, most people are not at the extremes.

"In Quad 1 is the Performer—High Technical but Low Tingle. This person does the job, yet that's all it is—a task with performance standards to meet. There's little passion or heart in it. Performers often say, 'Every day I go to work a bit of me dies.'"

"Ouch," said the man, "That's sad but I understand."

Bob resumed, "Prospects live in Quadrant 4 with their High Tingle and Low Technical. These people are committed to the cause even if they can't significantly contribute to the effort—yet. With technical training, Prospects have the potential to become TOP Performers.

"There are two ways to develop TOP Performers:

"1. Help Performers find their Tingle.

"2. Train Prospects to become more Technical.

"Prospects tend to be the richest, most consistent source of future TOP Performers, because learning Technical is taught where Tingle is caught. High-Tingle people are valuable. We work hard to find and keep High-Tingle people. They're special. Tingle trumps Technical in our book.

"Ideally, we want both qualities present. Yet, Technical alignment ebbs and flows due to new technologies, market shifts, and a host of other factors that create obsolescence. High-Tingle people are valuable even when their Technical alignment momentarily falters, for whatever reasons. We keep High-Tingle people in our TOP Prospect Pool. It's a safe haven to transition Prospects into TOP Performers. Typically, Prospects quickly become TOP Performers again in another role simply because their work matters."

The man chuckled as he said, "This sounds like competitive ice skating, where the competitors earn scores based on a combination of technical merit and artistic performance. The champion must excel in both to win."

"Exactly!" Bob affirmed. "Great analogy."

The man observed, "It occurs to me that there's a subtle yet profound distinction between the R. D. Scott Company and most businesses, including mine."

"What's that?" inquired Bob.

"In my business it isn't possible to have TOP Performers. We've failed to clearly articulate the purpose of our organization or how our work makes a difference. That keeps us one-dimensional — Technical only. On the other hand, your business is built around both dimensions with specific intention."

"Right," Bob answered. "I focus on integrating Technical and Tingle in our corporate culture. Tingle without Technical is daydreaming."

"I agree," the man conceded. "Most of us who run businesses have built them around the Technical and very lightly on Tingle. It places us at a strategic disadvantage."

Bob said, "Tingle is still obscure because the power of purpose is as yet unrealized. It keeps coming back to our heart." Again Bob placed his hand over his heart as he spoke. "In the business world especially, we speak too little about the heart. In fact, foolishly it is often downplayed, as are many things people don't understand."

The man defended the position. "Yes, but in the business world, coming from the heart implies an emotional and weak response. Business is logical and tough. That's just the way it is."

"Is it really?" Bob doubted. "On the contrary, coming from the heart or a place of purpose is absolutely the strongest place to be coming from. Changing someone's mind is easier than changing one's cause."

Bob continued, "Coming from the heart makes sense in life and in business. Long after the product or service is rendered, the feelings of the experience remain for the customer. Those feelings are the sense of alignment from both Technical and Tingle."

The man replied, "So the On-Purpose Principle is the touchy-feely stuff of business."

"Wrong," Bob corrected. "It is the very essence of business because businesses are ultimately people serving people. All the other stuff—the financial, marketing, legal, accounting, and so forth—are Technical functions supporting the path of purpose to the frontline of service. Tingle with customers, team members, and vendor partners are managed like any other resource.

"Because it's intangible, it's easy to overlook. But safe refuge in cold, hard numbers is folly. Ignore Tingle and you're managing to half the potential of the business in real terms."

"Half the potential!" the man exclaimed. "That's a bold statement. This is a new perspective for me. You know, 'Business is business.' That was one of Fred Taylor's favorite expressions."

"Yes, and 'All's fair in love and war,' right? Wrong! Please don't use those old clichés to justify unreasonable behaviors in the name of the holy grail of profit. They're simply trite excuses for harmful and unhealthy behaviors that wring the Tingle out of us.

"In the Industrial Age, just because some executives and managers got away with that attitude, it didn't make it right. People have always been the essential ingredient in business."

The man was struck by Bob's certainty on these matters. But Bob was right. "Business is business" had never been a satisfactory response, only a condescending putdown implying, *If you don't know any better, I'm not explaining it to you.* In on-purpose terms, it was a lost teachable moment.

Because of his long association with The Old Man, the man found himself using Fred's expressions far too often at work and at home. Thankfully Bob logically led him to realize the error of his ways. The On-Purpose Principle took root in his mind.

Sensing the man's brain was on overload, Bob Scott grinned. "Let's take a break. May I treat you to one of our world-famous chocolate chip cookies hot out of the oven?"

"Absolutely," said the man.

Bob called Dave, their waiter, to the table and placed the order. A plate of cookies arrived with two fresh cups of coffee. The aroma was devastatingly delicious. With the man's first bite of cookie, a string of melted chocolate goo fell to his lower lip and lapped onto his chin. He commented, "Um-mmm! These are great! Being off-purpose never tasted so good." Like two school kids at recess, they broke from their business conversation and chatted about families and favorite sports teams.

8
The On-Purpose Paradox

▼

Build the people, and the people will build the business.

Attributed to Brownie Wise
Innovator of the Tupperware home party

The chocolate chip cookies provided a needed break from their on-purpose business discussion.

The man probed for further clarity, "It seems that the *customer*, not the purpose or alignment, needs to be the focus of the business. A business that gets too inwardly focused risks becoming near-sighted. Where's the customer in this?"

"You're well-schooled in business," Bob commented and then paused to choose his next words. The man delighted in the compliment until Bob added, "Except that customer focus alone falls short of the mark."

"I don't get it," the man admitted. "Everything I read says that customer focus is the be-all and end-all for a business."

"I understand. They are a key piece of a whole service system," Bob stated matter-of-factly.

"How so?"

"An on-purpose business is designed and dedicated to serving. Recall that purpose statements begin with 'I exist to serve by....' The on-purpose paradox is that in serving the customer, you also serve your organization, your greater community, yourself, and God. It's a complete and wholesome cycle of service. Everyone wins or it's no deal."

"That's an extraordinary standard," protested the man.

"Tell me then," countered Bob, "Whom will you choose to deny serving? The customer? Your employees? Your executives? Your community? Yourself? Your family? God?" He added a caution, "Think before you speak."

Pondering Bob's question and warning, he knew the answer. Bob was right. Still he protested, "It's a matter of semantics. It's all one and the same."

Bob firmly held his ground. "You've missed the point. I've seen businesses so customer focused at the employees' expense that the employees were the walking wounded. The customer is happy with the transaction, but the employee is trashed. How long do you think an employee with options will stay on a job if day after day he's a customer doormat? Particularly if company policy dictates that 'the customer is always right.'"

The man acknowledged, "Not long, I imagine."

"Right. As a result, the company has high turnover, burnout problems, and high personnel costs for recruiting, training, and the like. In the end, customer service suffers because people are always worried about whether they'll have a job or if they want a job there. The primary directive of customer service ultimately erodes and undermines profits. The business fails, so the community loses an engine of economic development and employment. Crazy, isn't it?"

"Yes. Yet," the man persisted, "'the customer is always right' is a stalwart rule of thumb for doing business. How can you say it isn't right?"

"I simply said it misses the mark; it's an inadequate directive for leading a business. It has validity, yet it can't be unilaterally applied without serious negative consequences. The fact is, customers are often wrong and looking for the added value and advantage of better service. Being on-purpose is inclusive. The person serving is being served while serving another, which all serves a greater good. Think of it this way: TOP Businesses have TOP Customers."

"That makes sense," the man replied. "Is it always possible to have high alignment?"

Bob laughed. "Of course not. That's why Pillar Four is 'Doing More of What You Do Best More Profitably.' This pillar is about seeking ultimate service opportunities. Questions we frequently ask here are, What is our ultimate TOP Opportunity? Who are our customers? Why does serving them give us joy? Describe the service with words and pictures. What steps are needed? How does the customer respond? Clarifying one's TOP Opportunity is a powerful exercise." Bob added, "Pillar Three, the Service Model, will offer tremendous help."

Just then, Dave, the waiter, came to the table with a cordless phone. "Bob, excuse me. It's your secretary, Helen, with a phone call for your guest."

Dave handed the phone to the man who released the hold button. "Hello!" He listened briefly, then said, "Thanks, Helen. Go ahead and transfer the call." After a moment, the man said, "Hi, Jackie. What's up?"

"I knew you had your cell phone off for the meeting with Bob. Sorry to interrupt. Bad news," Jackie disclosed. "Fred Taylor was just rushed to the hospital from his home. Apparently, he's had another heart attack."

Excusing himself from Bob, the man took off for the hospital. As his car raced, so did his mind. He had a love-hate relationship with Fred. In one way The Old Man was like a protective father. Fred could also be neglectful and caustic. The man cared enough for Fred to be there for him, but on the other hand, he didn't understand why he was even bothering to go. Fred would have told him, "You can't afford to be making hospital calls on company time. Business is business."

The man gave a sad smile, thinking once again of Fred's motto. With Fred, the scorecard was always money. The man knew that money drives people only so far. Eventually they need their work to matter. Being treated as a cog in the wheel is degrading and deflating.

What a difficult manner of doing business, thought the man. His eyes were now open to his challenging work environment under Fred.

Building a business based upon strength of culture, service, openness, alignment, civility, and the heart was previously a foreign concept.

Heart! That sparked a thought about Fred's heart as he pulled into the hospital garage. After parking the car he paused for a calming moment behind the wheel. Considering The Old Man's "heart condition," he thought, *What is going through Fred's mind right now? As his life may be passing before him, are there regrets, unfulfilled dreams, or does he have peace?*

9
Pillar Two:
The *Think Inc!* Mindset

▼

Now is the time to recognize ... that for every right there is a
corresponding obligation,
for every choice there is a consequence.

Finola Bruton,
wife of Ireland's Prime Minister John Bruton (1994-1997)

Fred Taylor suffered congestive heart failure. The man had visited
with Mrs. Taylor, who was waiting in recovery. Unlike Fred, who
had a strong, driven personality, Mrs. Taylor was a gracious
woman with a quiet inner peace and strength. The man thought, *It
must be true: opposites attract.*

A week had passed since the man bolted from Bob to the
hospital. The man was anxious to resume his on-purpose business
mentoring. Bob Scott had arranged two meetings for him, one with
Frances Attwood and another with Hal Trudy.

Frances Attwood's name was instantly recognizable because it
was plastered on "For Sale" signs on homes all around town.
According to Bob, her mastery of Pillar Two— *Think Inc!*—had
transformed her career.

Arriving promptly at Bob's office, he was introduced to
Frances. His first impressions of her were that she showed high
energy, self-confidence, and smarts. Her ebony skin was smooth
and gave the impression of a much younger woman than her forty-
five years. On her nicely tailored suit she wore a gold lapel pin with
the words "On-Purpose."

"I like your lapel pin," the man remarked.

She responded with a laugh. "Thank you! You just reminded me to be on-purpose."

The man smiled. "That's clever."

Frances explained, "Every outfit I own has an on-purpose pin on it. In my business—hold that, in my life—there are a b-i-l-l-i-o-n distractions," she dramatically stretched her arms for effect, "drawing me off-purpose. Thanks to these little pins, I have an army of on-purpose partners." She winked and added, "For free."

Bob Scott observed, "You two will get along great." He inquired, "How's Fred?"

"Thanks for asking. Given the heart damage, Fred's health is fragile." They commiserated.

Turning to Frances, the man offered, "I'm excited to learn about Pillar Two."

Bob offered them the use of his conference room. "I'll be back shortly," he said. Then, turning to Frances, he said, "He's seeing Hal Trudy after your visit."

Frances's face lit up. "What an opportunity! I listed and sold Hal's house when he retired. He's a true gardener—loves to get his hands dirty."

Bob left as the two settled into chairs. Frances asked, "What do you know about Pillar Two?"

"Bob and I touched on it a while ago," answered the man. "Assume I know nothing."

"Great," said Frances. "Pillar Two is *Think Inc!*. It is an attitude and point of view where each person, regardless of one's job title, is the owner and president of his or her work. It means adding value and discovering ways to make profitable contributions. It means utilizing and controlling resources for creating products and services ... devising systems ... managing the environment ... leading when needed ... getting out of the way when not ... reframing the negatives into positives ... engaging people productively ... reconciling the long-term and the short-term. If I were to sum it up in a couple of words ..."

In concert, they both said, "... being responsible."

"Exactly," Frances affirmed. "And the opposite of responsibility is blame. If *Think Inc!* is assuming responsibility for one's thoughts, feelings, beliefs, time, and performance, then Stink Inc. is blaming and whining about everyone and everything. People with Stink Inc. are foul and to be avoided."

He chuckled and added, "Being responsible versus blaming. Absolutely! People who shoulder responsibility are special. Tell me more."

"*Think Inc!* is the essential mindset of the on-purpose business person. It's like the light switch. We have to want to turn it on. Responsibility requires ownership of the outcome. When the outcomes aren't favorable, it's simple to blame it on someone or some circumstance. People with *Think Inc!* know that negative outcomes aren't failures, they're learning experiences designed to spur our creativity. With blame, even the learning experience is lost."

Frances continued, "Some people believe *Think Inc!* doesn't apply to them. Discounting the business side of things is a big mistake! Every employee is really a solo owner running a business.

"In my industry, for example, there are real estate agents and brokers. When an agent defines herself by her job title she creates a self-limiting constraint. The *Think Inc!* agent, however, sees herself as a business person who own a real estate practice. This is a subtle yet vitally different point of view."

The man nodded his understanding, and Frances continued, "In this way the insurance agent doesn't run an agency, he runs a practice within a business. The receptionist runs a PR practice, not a switchboard. The delivery person operates a shipping and handling practice. With *Think Inc!* every person can run a practice: nurses, pastors, teachers, salespeople, assembly line workers. All own their book of business because they choose to assume greater ownership of their life and work." Frances paused, "... but most people don't."

"Why is that?" the man asked.

"Many are inadvertently in business. They began their careers trained with a technical skill, such as being a schoolteacher, lawyer, doctor, engineer, banker, artist, tradesperson, or so forth. Now they're running a business or a book of business. These accidental business persons are not formally prepared or trained to be in business so they don't know what they don't know. Lack of knowledge undermines their confidence. For some, the very thought of being a business person is distasteful, at best. This professional reluctance to embrace the business of being in business limits their possibilities.

"Owners, on the other hand, are thrust into *Think Inc!*. Risk and reward compels them to be more proactively engaged in learning the business of being in business.

"Employees, however, who just focus on the job at hand are one dimensional. A *Think Inc!* person sees the context of work to be adding value, doing what's best, selling, building a team, and being on-purpose."

The man agreed. "You're right. An employee mindset tends to be nearsighted and accepts what comes along. A person with the *Think Inc!* mindset finds and creates situations and opportunities above and beyond the technical job description. Their Tingle factor overflows.

"Presidents have to think strategically. In most businesses only a handful of people think, act, and decide with greater context. The alternative is to fall mindlessly in line—a self-appointed cog in the wheel."

Frances agreed. "Right! Imagine how engaging and powerful it is when everyone learns and uses the Four Pillars as the president of his or her own business—from entry-level new hires to top management. Imagine a company fully operating with *Think Inc!* people."

"The release of this much intellectual horsepower would be awesome," the man replied. "But I have a question. How do you get managers, let alone supervisors and frontline people, to organize like a business owner?"

Frances flashed a large smile. "That is what you'll learn with Pillar Three, the Service Model. Remember, *Think Inc!* is only one of the Four Pillars. Individually, each is potent. Combined, the whole is greater than the sum of the parts."

"I see," the man nodded.

What You Do Best

He continued, "Bob tells me that *Think Inc!* changed your life. How so?"

"The R. D. Scott Company regularly spins off affiliated businesses with team members and supports them in various ways. That's how my business got started. I was using *Think Inc!* and saw an opportunity outside the company to start a business."

"They just let you go?" asked the man.

Frances explained, "It was an incubation process. When I came to work here nine years ago in the personnel area, it was a much smaller, fast-growing business. We were hiring and relocating lots of people here. This is my hometown; I know e-v-e-r-y-b-o-d-y. I'm a natural connector.

"I loved relocating people here, and I saw an opportunity to start a relocation business. Bob and I talked about it, and he staked my business with his relocations and a *Think Inc!* mindset. My initiative paid off. Within days of securing my real estate license I had my first buyer's contract; I also had more fun and made more money than I did the entire month before. The rest is history."

The man sat on the edge of his seat in wonder. "In my company, your manager would have probably fired you for proposing your business idea as 'disloyalty' to the company."

Frances smiled. "I'm blessed to be here. If initiative is the stuff of presidents, then conformity is the stuff of Stink Inc. Bob and I both won and keep winning. Bob needed a great relocation service to grow his company because a failed relocation cripples the business and disrupts a family and career. By encouraging and supporting my business, we both excel at doing more of what we do best more profitably. Pretty logical, right?"

"Absolutely win-win," the man agreed.

"Bob placed two conditions on my departure. One: create the best relocation business possible. Done!

"Two: invite others to be on-purpose business persons, too. At first, I thought Bob was asking me to be altruistic. In a sense it is, but it is just a great business approach. I've helped launch or grow business for a local homebuilder, a property insurance agent, a home remodeler, a landscaper, a painter ... the list goes on and on. With all these great businesses, is our community a better place to live? Look around! Is my business better than my peers? Yes! Do you think I get referrals? By the handfuls!"

The man jumped in. "A sales force you don't pay — kind of like your on-purpose 'pin' pals, right?"

Frances laughed and nodded her agreement.

A knock on the conference room door was followed with Bob Scott emerging from behind it. "Have you mastered *Think Inc!*?" he cheerfully asked the man.

"Bob, I've only sat at the feet of the master of *Think Inc!*. Frances is great. *Think Inc!* is really about opening the minds and lives of people to explore their leadership possibilities. As one of the Four Pillars of an on-purpose business, this deep-seated sense of responsibility really hit home."

"I'd say you learned your lesson. Say goodbye to Frances, your on-purpose partner, and let's go see Hal Trudy."

The man thanked Frances. Their time together had been short, but her lesson would endure.

The Park Bench

Bob ushered the man into his office and outside through a set of double doors. Across the street from the R. D. Scott Company was a large public park with wonderful old trees and blooming flowers. Bob confided, "Often this park is my getaway from the office stress. I walk here at lunch to exercise and to clear my thoughts."

The fresh air and sun felt pleasant. The aroma of fresh-cut grass filled the air. A gardener pushed an ancient rotary-blade lawn mower on a small grassy knoll in the distance. The man delighted in the metal-upon-metal sharpening sound of the rotary blades snipping the blades of grass. It reminded him of simpler days. The gardener gave a friendly wave to Bob as they crossed the street. Bob returned the greeting.

The man appreciated Bob's investment of his time, expertise, and relationships. Meeting these respectable men and women offered hope that gracious acts of service remained the true gold standard in life and business. They approached a bench under the limbs of an ancient live oak tree. Bouquets of impatiens growing from terra cotta pots surrounded it. The man couldn't help but comment, "This is beautiful, and so peaceful."

"It's a special place. Have a seat," Bob said, offering the park bench. "I have a plane to catch. Hal will be along to see you and talk. Let's chat soon … after you've had time to absorb all you're learning."

They shook hands and Bob left for the airport. The man sat waiting for Hal.

10

Pillar Three:
The Service Model

▼

Rosebud!

The last word spoken by Citizen Kane
from the movie *Citizen Kane*

Admiring his surroundings, the man relaxed on the bench as he awaited the arrival of Hal Trudy. His peaceful interlude waned as a disturbing wind of thoughts blew in. *Things are bad at the business. Sales are dropping, morale is low, and production problems persist. The GEOMay contract is all but lost. We've got to act fast.*

The man stood and paced to a nearby rose garden in hopes of clearing his mind. Sniffing from rose to rose momentarily calmed the storms in his thoughts.

"Ah-h, you like my roses," came a kind voice from behind the man. He turned to see the gardener's proud smile.

"Is this your handiwork?" asked the man.

"I accept partial responsibility," said the gardener, pointing toward heaven. "I get lots of help from my Higher Authority. Roses of many varieties are my joy." He guessed the gardener to be in his mid-to-late seventies. His stride and movements appeared to be those of a much younger man. Up close, though, his age showed on a sun-worn face set with sparkling blue eyes and a flashing smile. A khaki city parks uniform covered his trim, fit body.

The man praised, "Your roses are beautiful!"

"Thank you. In caring for roses, I also care for myself."

The man said, "Thanks for this haven in the midst of a crazy world. I envy you. Your work makes a difference for people."

The gardener furrowed his brow. "And your work is not so meaningful and rewarding?"

The man swung his head in a resigned manner. "No need to burden you with my problems. I'm meeting a man here shortly. I'm trusting he will show me a better method."

"Sir, it's no burden. Liberating greatness within you keeps me on-purpose," said the grinning gardener as he extended his right hand. "Hi! I'm Hal Trudy, your appointment."

The man was embarrassed. Introducing himself, he apologized for his presumptuous behavior.

Hal answered, "Don't apologize; learn a lesson."

"Don't judge a book by its cover," the man suggested.

"Perhaps." Hal smiled. "The bigger lesson is to see your work as a beautiful expression of your purpose. Regardless of the humbleness of the duty performed, you can be on-purpose. All work is meaningful if we choose for it to be so.

"First, you must value your work regardless of the pay scale the world places on it. It is inherently profitable when it is on-purpose. Two thousand years ago a wise man posed the question, 'For what does it matter, if you gain the world, but lose your soul?'"

The man asked Hal, "What if my work causes me to lose my soul?"

"Only you can choose to lose your soul. Meaning is neither found nor lost in power, pleasures, position, or prestige. Purpose is first an attitude of the heart. Move toward your purpose, and TOP Opportunities steadfastly emerge."

Hal held the stem of a rosebud and snipped it from the bush. Handing it to the man, he continued, "We're like a fresh-cut rose. Life and time are perishable. The greatness of our spirit is enduring."

"Thank you for the advice," the man said. "By any chance, does your purpose statement involve roses?"

"Metaphorically, yes," Hal replied. "My purpose statement is 'Liberating Greatness.' You see, roses require cultivation and care to bloom. A rose holds greatness of beauty but it must be tenderly liberated from the earth and a thorny bush. Roses like people are designed to bloom brilliantly. Both need proper care, nourishment, pruning, and attention to exhibit such freedom to be. We all have such greatness longing to be liberated to make a difference. I do my best to nudge this along in rose bushes and people. Roses are my elegantly meaningful metaphor for humanity and me."

"I see. And you can liberate greatness everywhere and anywhere?" the man supposed.

"That's the plan. Some conditions and situations are more favorable than others for living one's purpose." Smiling now, Hal offered, "As in my little garden here, to improve conditions sometimes one deals with the fertile manure of experiences that smudge yet, shall we say, enrich our character." The men laughed.

The man was struck by this gardener's vitality, humor, and earthy wisdom. He invited Hal to join him on the bench under the magnificent oak. Then he said, "Please teach me about Pillar Three : The Method of the on-purpose business."

Hal picked up a broken oak twig and playfully maneuvered it from hand to hand while speaking. "The Method is the Service Model. This on-purpose prototype provides a systematic means to transform a purpose statement into an operational reality, that is, to be on-purpose." With that, Hal pointed his stick toward the man's chest as an old schoolmaster might do to a student and asked, "Ready to get started?"

"Yes, sir," snapped the man smartly.

The Service Model

"The Service Model is common sense." Hal half cupped his mouth with his hand, leaned toward the man, and whispered, "Unfortunately, common sense isn't so common these days." They both smiled.

Hal resumed his teaching. "How do you think the model got its name?"

"The Service Model?" asked the man. "Is this a trick question?"

"No, I assume nothing."

"The Service Model is about service," answered the man.

"Right," Hal confirmed. "Do you appreciate the importance of this relative to creating an on-purpose business?"

"I hadn't thought of the connection," the man replied.

"Is customer service important to your business?" Hal questioned.

"Of course it is. We're constantly working on improving customer service."

Hal stated, "I promise that the Service Model will prove to be illuminating for creating a healthier culture, more profitable business, and, by the way, significantly better customer experiences!

"Purpose is a service concept. Recall that the consistent start of a purpose statement is 'I exist to serve by ...' or, for an organization, 'We exist to serve by ...' and it is followed with a two-word purpose statement.

"Ask the average person or business person why a business exists and they'll likely tell you it exists to make a profit. That's correct only within the very narrow science of economics. Business is much more than that. First, business has a societal context; that means that people—employees, customers, and management—and the greater community matter. Here the premium is on service to people, and profit is an essential by-product resulting from adding value to relationships. People and profit must both be present or the venture is off-purpose. For a business to be sustainable and on-purpose, relationships with people are held as more valuable than the transaction itself. The transaction is simply an exchange of value within the relationship."

The man's eyes opened wide. "This is different."

Hal agreed, "Yes, radically different. Service is purpose in action. Even businesses that are customer service-minded may miss the mark. They typically talk in terms of customer service. Actually there are three tests of service. First, does the organization serve a greater good or higher power? Second, does the person providing the service gain from the act of serving? Third, does it serve to create value for others, i.e. the customers? For the business to be on-purpose we need to hear 'yes' to all three questions."

"That's a high standard," the man said.

"Yep!" said Hal emphatically as the final word on the point. He brought the question full circle with a rhetorical question, "So why is it called the Service Model?"

The man repeated, "Purpose is a service concept."

"Good, but think more," prompted Hal. "What's a model?"

The man said, "A model is a set of plans, a design, a pattern, or prototype for others to follow. It's a scaled miniature of something larger, like a model airplane. It's an ideal version, like a model citizen."

"Yes," Hal agreed. "In fact, the Service Model is all those definitions. Now put it together: service *and* model."

"I get it," the man said. "The Service Model is a plan or design for putting purpose into action with people. It is also a pattern for others to follow so they can duplicate it. And it's a miniature of something larger. It's an ideal to strive toward."

"Terrific," Hal commended.

The man continued, "If that's true, then the Service Model is a strategic, tactical, and operational tool enabling more predictable execution of service that profits all. That would create more efficiencies and effectiveness as well as scalability, wouldn't it?"

Hal stood up from the park bench and stretched his hands high in the air. "Excellent! You've got it. Let's take a stroll. I need to make my rounds with rose bushes in another part of the park." They walked.

Hal continued, "Like learning anything new, you'll need to invest time and practice to master it. If you need some extra coaching, you know where I work. As you master the Service Model, you'll more consistently render model service." Hal gave an impish grin and winked. "A little play on words."

11
The Service Levels

▼

Some people walk in the rain. Others just get wet.

Roger Miller
Singer and Songwriter

As the two men strolled the park grounds, the man reflected on his lessons. The Service Model, as Hal described it, was still just a concept that seemed almost too simple and sensible to be useful. Having no mental image of it, he struggled to relate. He broached the topic with Hal.

"Is there actually such a thing as the Service Model?"

Hal turned and smiled at him. "I thought you'd never ask. Give me a minute to check these rose bushes for insects and mites." As Hal inspected the bushes, he told the man, "Mites are one of many tiny little critters that can infect a rose bush. They can kill the bush or stifle the production and quality of buds and blooms." Businesses, like roses, require constant and intensive care and feeding to prevent pests and other vermin from pulling them down.

"The Four Pillars of the on-purpose business made me a wealthy man. They can do the same for you but you've got to be willing to tend the garden. Remember the difference between being rich and being wealthy. Riches are in the pockets, and wealth is in the heart. I'm blessed with both."

Hal placed his arm affectionately around the man's shoulder. "Many people don't understand business. Greed, cutthroat behaviors, and ill treatment of people are bad business and bad for business. Business is a high and noble calling in which you risk much to give much. Finance, marketing, operations, and all that — they're functions or disciplines within business. Business is about people organized to profit society through innovation and the lowering of costs so standards of living are raised. Implied is a moral basis. In practice, morality isn't always present, but that's the human condition that's been with us since the first garden.

"Today, you have a growing awareness and more insights. Mastering the model invites a further investment and experience with it. You're in insightful ignorance — now you know what you didn't know before."

The man felt some relief and encouragement. "So, show me the Service Model already."

"Sure. We start with five Ps — they're the progressive and iterative steps to building the Service Model. With these you'll have the ABCs — to analyze, build, and correct the business. The Five Ps in order are: Purpose, Plan, People, Processes, and Performance, all to serve the Customer and the Customers' Customers and so forth."

Hal knelt to the ground and used his stick as a writing tool. The man dropped to one knee beside him. To an onlooker they looked like two sandlot football players drawing plays in the dirt.

Hal wrote a large triangle in the dirt. "This is the Service Model. Two of the legs create a large V that represents 'Values' or the boundaries for business decisions. At the base of the V let's write 'Purpose,' representing the purpose of the organization. Next, we'll fill in the other Ps."

The Service Model

As Hal finished sketching it, the man bid him, "I'm fascinated. Keep talking."

"First," Hal instructed, "We start at the bottom of the Service Model. That's contrary to the usual focus of most managers who press for better performance. The Service Model provides a deeper context and understanding to the roots of performance. One can't expect an abundance of roses if the roots and bush aren't tended. Performance for the Customer is on the surface. Instead, let's get below the surface.

"Purpose — this is the organizational seed where the On-Purpose Principle (Pillar One) connects. State the purpose of the organization as 'P(o).' The On-Purpose Principle links to the Service Model. Without the leader's purpose informing and energizing the Service Model, it is simply a structure with no heart to pump it and no vision to inspire it to greatness. It's an empty suit.

"Plan — an on-purpose plan includes vision(s), missions, and values emanating from a single organizational purpose. This positions the company to occupy a place in the mind of the customer. It's very important. Remember to include simple strategic, operational, and tactical plans that inform day-to-day execution or performance. Include key outcomes and goals as well. In fact, a good plan is simply a Service Model in the design stage.

"People—you need a team to engage with the purpose and plan. Ideally, they are Quadrant 2 leaders: TOP Performers. When on-purpose persons are working in an on-purpose business, it is downright magical. Identify not just what you need technically, but find the Tingle that turns on their light switch.

"Processes—here's where efficiency and scalability are created. These are the functional disciplines such as finance, marketing, people, and operations. Do you want to know what processes are most valued in a business? Look at the titles in the executive suite. They're usually described by function, such as Vice President of Marketing or Chief Financial Officer. Decide what processes you want to value and name them wisely for they create the structure and language that support performance.

"Performance—The prior 4 Ps set up Performance for success or failure. In this level the mission of the business comes to life as people do their jobs and bring expression to the purpose. Key Performance Indicators (KPIs) measure the output and productivity against set standards and stated expectations. Ultimately, the work of the business needs to happen and here's where the day-to-day action happens.

"Front Line—The line between the Customer and Performance is the proverbial "Front Line" of the business where the business visibly blooms. All direct customer contact takes place at the top of the Performance level within the Service Model. This interface of the inside and outside of the business creates the customer experience. Company front line team members are salespeople, receptionists, delivery people, customer-service personnel, accounts payable, and others whose work has direct customer contact.

"Customer—for us to be on-purpose, we serve customers, clients, patients, guests, or whatever noun is appropriate to the organization. Serving customers is the lifeblood of a business and the ultimate expression of its purpose. Customers (C1) are the outward and visible recipients of an inner-rewarding service rendered; and that's called being on-purpose. Not shown on this model are the Customers' Customers. The better you understand your Customers' Customers (C2) or your Customers' Customers' Customers (C3), the better you can design and deliver for your Customer. This chain of customers also informs improvements to the Service Model.

"There you have the Five Ps of the Service Model. To borrow a term from biology, it is a living molecule for inspiring, creating, building, improving, and multiplying an organization. Each service level predictably relates to the next. It's as natural as acorns producing oaks. The Service Model borrows from nature's growth process."

The man responded, "If I understand it correctly, every performance-related issue in a business actually has roots in the purpose of the organization."

"Exactly," Hal commended. "A business is like a rose bush. In other words, roses don't bloom unless the roots, bush, and stems are healthy. The entire system requires cultivation to produce the growth and buds.

"In contrast, consider a business that starts wanting 'flowers' but won't feed the plant or prepare the soil. That's a business focused on the Performance level only. This 'showy' short-term thinking style of business with shallow roots can actually work ... for a while! But these are false results. The plant can't endure hardships, and the harvest will be scarce."

Alignment and Integration

Hal pressed the man, "Now that you're aware of the Service Model, how might you start a business?"

"I would ... wow!" the man interrupted himself. "This is a unique vantage point. I would define the purpose of the organization by completing the phrase 'I exist to serve by ...' and write my two word purpose statement. I would check this in terms of how to make a difference for the Customer, the community, the team, and me. It needs to be meaningful work and stated as such.

Then I would create a vision for the company and a positioning with our customers that would feed into the plan to be on-purpose."

Hal nodded approvingly as the man pointed his finger into the dirt to the People level.

"Next, I would gather a team to help make the Plan a reality and to put the Processes in place to perform for the customers. My team and I would think through our customer chain to understand their needs and value expectations."

"Excellent!" Hal approved. "One more question for you to ponder. How does strategy fit with being an on-purpose business?"

A stream of thoughts erupted from the man, "The Service Model ... Purpose is a service concept ... the Five Ps ... plus the Customers ..."

The man's face lit up in recognition. "I've got it. Alignment! The entire organization is aligned with the purpose of the organization; that's an on-purpose business. Then, the Five Ps are aligned to serve the C1, C2, and C3 Customer. As a result, the business is on-purpose, rather than off-purpose. I guess you might say even the Customers are on-purpose."

"Yes, you nailed it!" congratulated Hal.

The man added, "It's an amazingly different and organic approach. It even feels healthier and more wholesome. Maybe the design and order are what make it all seem so manageable. In all my years in business, this makes the big picture simpler and easier to visualize."

Hal's eyes twinkled with a mentor's delight. The man, in fact, understood a great deal of the Service Model prior to their meeting. He had just never had a platform to organize his leadership and management. Hal knew the next lesson would stretch the man even further.

"In the beginning, you may recall, I said the Service Model is in the shape of a V for values. In addition to having values, an on-purpose business also adds value. Your company is facing survival issues right now. In these times, it is so tempting to take shortcuts.

Don't! Use the Service Model to rapidly reorganize the scattered pieces into a cohesive mosaic.

"Earlier, you touched on a vital point: TOP Customers. You need to meet a dynamo of a woman. Her name is Pam Dimes. She's a value-adding natural. Listen to her. You need what she has to share to turn around the company. Call her." He handed the man Pam's business card. "She's a business owner. After you meet Pam we'll visit some more. Deliberate on what you've learned and how to put this into practice in your company."

"Thanks, Hal. I will. I had never really considered business design before. Now I can!"

They shook hands. Hal returned to his work in the rose garden.

The man called Pam and arranged an appointment for the following week.

▼ ▼ ▼

Back in his office the man sat at his desk writing in the pages of his journal. Order was emerging from chaos.

He contemplated the On-Purpose Principle, *Think Inc!*, and the Service Model. *What are the future implications of this new approach? How do I put all I've learned into practice? How do I get everyone in the company to use the On-Purpose Pillars? Becoming an on-purpose business will be a tough shift in our corporate culture and method of operation. This change,* he thought, *is needed and will actually bring us back to our roots. No pun intended.*

A knock on his open door broke his thoughts. Jackie popped her head into his office and said, "Mrs. Taylor is on the phone."

Raising the phone to his ear, he greeted his former boss's wife. "Hi, Mrs. Taylor. How's Fred?"

In a soft voice she answered, "It's his heart again. I'm at the hospital. I wanted you to know since you were kind enough to visit last time. He's not taking visitors right now so no need to interrupt your day."

"Is he all right?" the man asked politely.

Mrs. Taylor's voice broke. "It's serious. Please invite any employees in the company to pray for him. To Fred, they're family."

She continued, "Our children are here and helping. I'm staying by Fred until he's alert. He'll want to talk. Despite his failing health, these are happy days for us. In the short time since his retirement he's become a free man without the burdens of the company weighing on him."

They exchanged goodbyes. He hung up the phone. A strange set of emotions whirled inside him. Fred worked all his life only to have his heart fail a few weeks after retiring. And Fred's "burdens" were now his! This wasn't the way the man wanted it to be for him. Something had to change! Something better change or the same fate awaited him.

Jackie walked into his office. "Is Fred okay?" she asked.

"No. He's back in the hospital." He asked Jackie to spread the word about Mrs. Taylor's prayer request.

12
Customer Confluence

▼

Wisdom is the art of living skillfully in whatever actual conditions
we find ourselves.

Eugene H. Peterson
The Message: Proverbs

Jackie announced to the man, "Pam Dimes is here to see you."

"Thanks!" The man headed to the lobby to greet Pam. The week since his meeting with Hal Trudy had flown by quickly. Fred was home recovering but weak.

As he walked, the man considered that his company was in bad shape and getting worse. Stress was high all around. Earlier in the week an executive team meeting had ended with an argument between Sam Cellars, the vice president of sales and marketing, and Pat Squires, the vice president of operations. He thought, *Perhaps Ms. Dimes has answers to help me focus the team on matters at hand.*

Spotting Pam in the lobby was easy. She was a striking sight in her bright red, tailored business suit. Set against her white pleated blouse was a tasteful gold necklace. They introduced themselves. While showing her to his office, the man inquired, "Please tell me about your business."

Pam began, "I'm an independent distributor with a direct sales company. I've built a large team over the years."

"Really!" he remarked in amazement. "Direct sales? Those aren't real businesses. So why would Hal want me to visit with you?"

Pam smiled at the man's comment because she knew all to well the prejudice against direct sales. She took it in stride and offered, "Perhaps Hal doesn't share your assessment of direct sales and because we might learn something from one another. Hal calls me a 'value-adding natural' so I imagine he wants me to share some insights with you."

Arriving at his office, he introduced Pam and Jackie. "Please hold my calls, Jackie." Pam and the man settled into chairs across from each other at a small round table in the corner. He asked, "So why does Hal call you a 'value-adding natural'?"

"Because I've got it figured out," Pam confidently offered.

"How so?" asked the man.

"Which of your customers are your TOP Customers—the most on-purpose for your business?" she quizzed.

"It depends," the man answered. "A lot of factors come into play."

Pam stopped him with her hand. "Excuses! I don't let my team members get away with that and I won't let you dance around it. Who are your on-purpose customers? They're the ones receiving the highest value for your product or service. An on-purpose business person must be able to pinpoint his or her best customers with high accuracy."

The man was intrigued with Pam's confidence and leadership. "How?" the man asked.

"Look at your Service Model. It was designed to serve a specific set of customers."

"We don't really have one, yet" the man answered. "We treat all customers the same."

"Then you have a Service Model by default," Pam informed. "Customers value your products and services differently. While you may not distinguish one customer from another, they distinguish your business from others every time they buy ... especially from a competitor."

"Ouch! I see," said the man. "So our Service Model gears us to be more suited to some customers than others."

"Exactly," Pam affirmed.

"So how do I get more of 'our' type of customers?" asked the man.

Pam beamed. "Excellent question. The phenomenon of 'our type of customers' is called Customer Confluence. It happens when high need intersects with excellence of execution."

The man joked, "The On-Purpose Prospect meets the On-Purpose Provider."

"Precisely," Pam indicated and added, "That's clever!"

"Thanks. But how?" the man asked again.

Pam explained, "Every level in the Service Model is a prelude to Performance for the Customer. In my business, our Purpose, Plan, People, and Processes are all geared to serve a specific customer segment. When that customer appears, no one, I repeat, no one is able to offer comparable value. The value of our performance depends upon our preparation. The Service Model is our preparation to profitably serve the TOP Customer.

"Think about when you've shopped for a service or product. Have you ever found a doctor whose expertise and manner matched your needs? Or maybe your wife found that perfect dress for a special occasion. Or was it finding the right school for a special-needs child? Consider what it was like when you finally found what you were looking for."

The man answered, "Joy, relief, good fortune, peace ..." Pam encouraged him with quick hand motioning to keep verbalizing his thoughts. "My needs were understood, even anticipated, and met."

"Were you willing to pay a premium if necessary?" she asked.

"Absolutely! I very well may have but it was a bargain by comparison to an open-end situation."

She continued, "And, assuming your customer experience met your expectations, did you tell anyone about it?"

He chuckled, "Yes, for a period of time, I told anyone who would listen."

"That," said Pam with authority, "is Customer Confluence. And when more of your customers experience the feelings you've just described, then you'll be well on your way to leading an on-purpose business."

The man supposed, "And without Customer Confluence ... all that's left as a basis of determining the value is price. Right?"

"Exactly. And price is an essential aspect of any transaction. So again I pose the question: Who are your TOP Customers?"

"I need to get with my people. I can't answer that question."

Pam encouraged him. "Once you can articulate who they are, what they want, and what they do, then you'll serve them like no other. Eventually they will become your best referral source for more customers like themselves because you provide the best value-added service or product."

The man observed, "I realize now that our company has a certain set of customers with whom we consistently excel. To fully leverage our investment in the Service Model, we need more of 'our kind of customers.' The on-purpose ones."

"Yes!" Pam enthused. "It makes no sense to keep on reinventing your Service Model to satisfy a revolving door of onetime customers. Now you can fully utilize your Technical and Tingle alignment with your customer chain (C1–C3). Customer Confluence results in repeat business and referrals because high value is embedded throughout the Service Model, all the way from the Purpose to the front line with and through the customer chain. This is the business equivalent of a divine appointment." Interlocking her fingers from both hands, she dramatically announced, "Finally, we've found one another!"

The man sat back in his chair. "Wow! I've never heard it expressed like that. You're right; it can be a magical moment, almost romantic."

"That's why we on-purpose business persons look to our Customers' Customers for further understanding of how we can best serve and add value. When we solve our customers' problems with their customers, then we make them heroes. That's value-adding beyond the sale."

The Front Line

Pam continued, "Many people talk about the front line of the business. We're going to define it as the line on the Service Model between the Customer and the Performance levels. Front line employees work in direct contact with customers.

"Everything in the Service Model is a prelude to Performance along the front line. Customer value is either gained or lost along the front line. Ideally, the customer's interaction with the front line is seamlessly smooth because of Customer Confluence. When that happens, it's like you're manufacturing customers."

"Manufacturing customers?" he queried.

"Not manufacturing like you're thinking of it. Remember, we're talking about adding value. Manufacturing, as I'm using it, means creating predictable, desired outcomes from a certain set of inputs and processes."

"Okay, that makes sense," he agreed.

"Good." She smiled. "The on-purpose business is like a precise Swiss watch. Hidden behind the face of the watch are movements, gears, and jewels hard at work. Watches must be predictably accurate. An on-purpose business via the Service Model provides similar reliability."

"Impressive, but is it realistic?" he questioned.

"Realistically, we're enhancing predictability, not creating certainty. Machines and watches can be crafted to tight tolerances. People, well," she joked, "they're often not so tolerable."

"Point well taken," conceded the man with a laugh.

Pam continued, "Customer Confluence is all about enabling each party in the relationship and transaction simply to do more of what they do best more profitably."

"Pillar Four!" The man recognized the phrase.

"Yes, Pillar Four," Pam confirmed.

The man pressed, "Go back for a second. You mentioned relationship and transaction. How do they relate to Customer Confluence?"

Pam explained, "Good question. The exchange of value is created in two ways: the transaction and the relationship. Ideally, value is high from both."

"What do you mean by transaction?" questioned the man.

"The transaction is the deal. It's the act of doing business — the contract, sale, or engagement for a product or service in exchange for consideration, monetary or otherwise. Typically, this is easily identified."

"And," asked the man, "how does relationship influence value?"

"Relationship is the feeling before, during, and long after the transaction is complete. It is more difficult to gauge directly."

"So," concluded the man, "if there's high Customer Confluence, then there's value added by both the transaction and the relationship. Right?"

"Right," Pam affirmed. "In plain English, it's a good deal for everybody and remains that way long after the transaction."

She proceeded, "Would you prefer to call on a customer cold or with a referral?"

"A referral, any day," he answered.

"Why?"

"It's a definite advantage because trust can more readily be established."

"And is trust valuable?" Pam asked.

"Absolutely," the man agreed and laughed. "You're good. I see how relationships add value to the transaction."

Pam acknowledged the compliment. "Thank you."

The man admitted, "Our front line team members are at a disadvantage because they don't have the benefit of a clearly defined Service Model supporting their efforts. In essence, we've undermined their best efforts because the root of our challenge lies deeper in the Service Model. Now I know where and how to enhance our Performance. These *are* potent insights."

Pam beamed with pride. "You're welcome," she said. "I figured a person in your position knew everything about business. I'm flattered a direct seller like me could help a big wig like you."

He rolled his eyes and said, "You'd be surprised what I've been learning. Hal was right. You are a value-adding natural. Customer Confluence sums it all up neatly.

"Thanks again for coming." The man walked Pam to the lobby and said goodbye.

▼ ▼ ▼

The Appointed Time

As the man returned from the lobby, Jackie reminded him, "You're late for your 'appointment.'"

Looking at his watch, he gasped. "I lost track of the time!" he said. "Please, call Jay, Tom, and Betty at Birdwood. Let them know I'm on my way. We're having lunch first, then playing eighteen. I'm gone."

Jackie laughed. "I know the routine," she said. "I'll take care of everything. Go!"

He ran to his car. This regular monthly golf foursome was made up of the company's commercial banker, CPA, and insurance agent. Shortly after being tapped as company president, he gathered these outside advisors to integrate their relationships of trust. So far it was working.

Wheeling his car from the parking lot, he fixed his mind on Customer Confluence. It was an eye-opening concept.

At the country club, a woman in a white minivan loaded with kids pulled out of a parking space right by the door to the men's locker room. He grabbed the space, dashed in, and changed into his golf clothes. Quickly he joined the others at the grill for lunch. Ever-thoughtful Jackie had gone the extra mile and ordered him a chef salad. He and the salad arrived at the same time. He was back on schedule.

They finished lunch and moved to the first tee. It was a sunny, perfect day for golf. The foursome had a great time while chatting business. The man was thrilled with the way he played. For a hacker, he scored a rare birdie on number five and had six pars.

Never mind the ten on number eight and the triple bogeys on numbers twelve and sixteen. He was having a rare afternoon away from the office. What a relaxing joy!

Walking off number eighteen, the golf pro emerged from the pro shop. "Your assistant, Jackie, called. Knowing that you turn off your cell phone when you play, she asked that you call her as soon as possible. It's important. She left her home phone number."

Taking the message slip, he said, "Thanks." Turning to his playing partners he said, "I need to make a quick emergency phone call. I'll see you in the 19th hole shortly."

Heading into the men's locker room, he dialed Jackie's number. It rang twice and then he heard "Hello." Jackie's voice lacked her typical perkiness.

He said, "Hi! It's me. What's up?"

"Bad news. Fred Taylor died this afternoon," Jackie said. "Fred's son called the office to let you know. There was nothing you could do, so I figured you might as well enjoy your golf game. I hope you don't mind."

"You did the right thing, Jackie." Hanging up the phone, he sank into a bench before the lockers. With his head in his hands tears welled up in his eyes. Despite all of Fred's shortcomings, he was The Old Man, the patriarch of the company, and a legend in the community. Their relationship spanned more than fifteen years. Fred alive offered him a measure of comfort as an occasional mentor and friend.

His heart ached. Never anticipating this emotional response, he realized that things were different; he was changing. The full burden of the business was truly on his shoulders now. The legendary Frederick W. Taylor was dead.

Gathering his thoughts he called Jackie back. "Thanks for tracking me down. Do you know the details of the funeral? Let's get the word out across the company."

13
The Model Way

▼

When one door of happiness closes, another opens;
but often we look so long at the closed door
that we do not see the one which has been opened.

Helen Keller (1880–1969)
Deaf and Blind Activist

A week had passed since Fred's death. The man spied Hal Trudy raking leaves near an azalea cluster down a path leading to a canopy of oaks, magnolias, and pines. "Hello!" he shouted to Hal.

Looking up from his work, Hal recognized him. They greeted and shook hands.

"Sorry to hear about Fred Taylor," Hal sympathized.

"Thanks. He was buried three days ago. The funeral was surprisingly uplifting. The pastor called it a resurrection service. The church was decked out in white. Even Mrs. Taylor wore a white dress!

"We sang some inspiring songs. I remembered 'Onward, Christian Soldiers' from my childhood when my parents took me to church. Another one was 'I Sing a Song of the Saints of God.' It has a catchy hook." He crooned the words.

Hal picked up the line to create an off-key duet: "... and one was a soldier, and one was a priest, and one was slain by a fierce, wild beast. And all of them were saints of God, and I hope to be one, too."

"You know it!" the man declared with amazement.

"Good stuff," Hal proclaimed, then added, "music is not my gift, though. Ain't nothing in 'liberating greatness' about singing."

After a chuckle, the man mused, "Fred's funeral was different. I expected ... well, you know, a funeral ... dark, somber, and sad. The sense of hope and renewal was a sharp contrast from the life of the Fred Taylor I knew." They chatted a bit longer about it.

Now leaning on his rake, Hal commented, "Fascinating. Maybe Fred finally began living in the midst of his dying. That's the Easter message, isn't it? There's always hope, no matter how bleak the situation appears."

Hal lamented, "Too bad. If only more people would choose the path of hope and choose it sooner. What will you learn from Fred's life, death, and service?"

The man didn't understand. Yet he knew Hal meant him well. From this reflective and uncomfortable question, he dodged a response. "Pam Dimes really helped me. Customer Confluence focuses the Service Model and makes it even more strategic and valuable. At my business we've spent so much time fixing symptoms that I never realized the systematic nature of our problems. All of our quick fixes created a variety of side effects that spawned a book of policies and procedures. Between government regulations and our own policy manual, we're bureaucrats, not business persons. We're way off-purpose.

"Because we don't know our TOP Customer, we're unfocused and a mess! With the Service Model I have a schematic to build and align from the foundational purpose of the business to the customer chain and every layer in between."

"Great," Hal said with a smile. "Have you learned anything else?"

"Customer Confluence fascinated me. With our limited resources we can't afford to build a Service Model for every conceivable customer. So I'm focusing our efforts on The On-Purpose Customers. We'll build our Service Model to serve them. It will demand pruning, but it's bound to be more rewarding than our current confused operation.

"I'm beginning with the GEOMay Company, our largest customer. We've fouled up that relationship."

"You're learning your lessons well," Hal commented.

The man thought, *Hal's so forthright and positive. What a great guy. I can't imagine what my career would have been like if I had worked for a person like him.*

Pods of Purpose

By then Hal was into a new thought. "There's another aspect to the Service Model," he said. "I'm going to ask you a question, and promise me you'll think for thirty seconds before you answer."

The man nodded his agreement.

"How many seeds are in an apple?"

The man started to answer, but Hal motioned for him to wait. The time passed, and then Hal called for the answer.

"I don't know." The man guessed, "… about ten."

Hal shook his head. "You're in your short-term, cash, and transactional mindset rather than a long-term, equity, relationship mindset. *Think Inc!* Try again."

The man thought for a few moments. Finally, he said, "Hal, hand me the stick so I can whack myself." Hal chuckled. The man realized, "An apple holds unlimited seeds. One seed in an apple could become another apple tree, which in turn produces more apples with seeds, which in turn produce more trees, more apples, more seeds, and the cycle goes on and on forever."

"Yes!" exclaimed Hal victoriously. "Yes. You're making progress. Building an organization is the same way. The Service Model is like a seed. So how many 'seeds' are in a business?"

"Unlimited," answered the man.

"Yes, and purpose is the germ of the seed. Most people have a pretty good idea of how plants grow; yet few people understand how an organization grows." Hal's speech quieted to a near whisper. "The fact is that leaders often lack the diversity and quantity of experience through the organizational development process. They think it is linear rather than cyclical so it is hard to recognize the larger pattern at play. The value of experience, mistakes, observation, and time is the emergence of recognized patterns."

The man moved nearer to Hal and said, "So, like a seed, the Service Model potentially holds an unlimited number of other Service Models. It's a manageable miniature for the growth process?"

"Yes," Hal confirmed. "The business has a Service Model and every person in the business has one as well. The only difference is scope of responsibility. The CEO has broader responsibilities than a sales representative; yet each person has his or her own Service Model within the company Service Model."

The Same Page

"So the Service Model provides a structural standard?" posed the man.

"Absolutely," Hal assured. "That's just one dimension, however. Beyond being a model, it is also a method for leaders to build team members and cohesive teams. Rather than replace experience, it enhances it with team and individual gains in perspective, guidance, and context."

The man said, "I'm not sure I understand."

"How many times have you said or heard it said, "We all need to get on the same page"?

Chuckling the man admitted, "Lots! Lately that's one of my favorite expressions because we are at such cross purposes."

"Listen closely," Hal implored, "This is important. The Service Model is 'the page' that can transform an overused expression into a rare reality."

The man gasped and his eyes widened with this epiphany. "Everyone really can be on the same page! Oh my God! If our people learn this model and method, then we can have a company full of *Think Inc!* team members who share a common language, perspective, and approach to building the business.

"Hal, as I think about the cost of being confused about the words of purpose, vision, mission, and values, then I'm struck even more by the sheer enormity of the price of not being 'on the same page.' There isn't an item on our income statement or balance sheet that isn't adversely affected.

"It's no wonder we're struggling. At headquarters we've been confused strategically and structurally. It is as if we, the executives, have conspired to confuse our employees and then layered policy after policy on top of them to conform to certain behaviors. How can they align to the purpose of the organization when none exists or is communicated? How can they *Think Inc!* when their entrepreneurial efforts have no corporate context? How can they engage and deliver world-class performance when their work is reduced to industrial age tasking instead of being tied to meaningfully making a difference?

"We're an off-purpose business because we're a company filled with people who are off-purpose at work because our culture fails to create, stimulate, and reward right behaviors. Our team members are well-intended but not well-supported. Am I right?"

Leaning against his rake, Hal smiled with delight and affirmed with a simple "Yes."

The man was awed. He said, "Here I am the president of this company, and so much of this is virgin territory for me. I can tell you where I've been, but having a model for where I am and we are going has always been challenging. My entire career I've bounced along without the benefit of a method for being in business. It's been business and career mostly by trial and error. I've stumbled and felt my way along trying not to offend. I was promoted not for boldness of thought and innovation, but for making fewer mistakes rather than better decisions. Playing it so safe doesn't come close to our potential to create value for customers, profits for our shareholders, and a better community."

"How sad never to be bold," Hal said with a sigh. "Both defense and offense are important. Fix these structural matters that are under your control while focusing on what matters most— developing your people as leaders of their lives and work."

The man reflected, "That would be amazing! On rare occasions someone special put an arm around me. These are mentors: Mrs. Ift, my third-grade teacher; Mr. Stifler, my eighth-grade math teacher; and Mr. Davies, who just encouraged me. The Professor has made a huge difference in my life. A retired business executive, Perry James, meets with me regularly, too. Of course my parents were the best. You've been amazingly giving and helpful. All of you saw my promise and potential before I did because you've had perspectives and experiences I didn't have. You've all elevated my sights.

"Hal, someone like Fred Taylor — shouldn't he have figured this out?"

"Fred Taylor didn't figure it out," Hal replied. "Stop blaming him, Mr. Stink Inc. He was what he was in his day. Frederick W. Taylor is dead, and so are his ways. Must we bury him again? Learn from the past, then move on. I'm sorry to have to be so blunt."

"Thank you," the man said. "I needed to hear that."

Hal stated, "There's a predictable pattern to business persons like Fred. Forty-eight seasons in the business taught him plenty. Give him credit for that. The problem was, only Fred knew what he knew. He was a master of the Technical and a neophyte of the Tingle. His forty-eight years on the job enabled him to declare solutions to problems, to be the answer man. He failed to develop those around him. Because his solutions were limited to his experiences, his stagnation confined the business to mediocrity.

"His focus was isolated to the Process and Performance levels. His idea of planning was setting sales goals and doing budgets. Fred felt he knew better than the Customer. How am I doing so far?"

"Yes. You're absolutely right," the man marveled. "Keep going."

"Goals and budgets are Performance-level activities, outcomes of what was set up by other Ps of the Service Model. Fred managed by objectives but never got to the object of the objectives — the purpose of the business is to serve people, not to minimalize them by making them into conforming cogs of the corporate machinery. Fred wasn't alone in this manner of business. In fact, he personifies the Industrial Age mindset and method.

"To Fred, the business was the numbers and operations. His blind spots were the people, plan, and purpose of the business. He was a 'get it done' driver with presidential responsibility, but not acting as an on-purpose president. He had no idea what he didn't know. For Fred, business life was a series of daily crises and burdens with only one predictable outcome," Hal reported.

"What's that?" asked the man.

"A heart attack."

"Ouch! Sad but true," agreed the man.

Hal nodded and asked, "What if Fred had known what you now know, and had acted on it?"

"Unbelievable," said the man, shaking his head. "Unbelievable where we might be today."

Hal added, "The Service Model enables more meaningful teachable moments, which grow both the person and the business. Each person can see on the model where he or she fits and how their contribution matters. Isolation and inadequacy give way to competence and confidence. It enables faster and better decisions to real situations and constant learning at every level of responsibility."

"You're right!" the man exclaimed.

Hal recognized that the concepts of an on-purpose business were taking root in the man.

"The Service Model is powerful," the man continued. "It's like having a mental filing cabinet where you place and retrieve information and insight at will. You now possess a permanent mental plan for organizing the organization."

"Yes," the man answered, "It's powerful."

The Nesting Dolls

The man continued. "The Service Model reminds me of those Russian nesting dolls. Pop the doll open and inside is a slightly smaller, similar doll. And inside that doll is a still smaller doll, and so on and so on."

"Yes," Hal laughed. "I love the image. The Service Model has nesting. The corporation has a Service Model. Open up the corporate model, and inside there's a nesting division model. Inside the division model is a business unit model, inside the business unit model is a department model, and inside the department model is a hard-working person with a position model. All are ideally and ultimately linked to and integrate with a common purpose and set of values."

"It's awesome," the man commented. "This is an insightful perspective on the business. Everyone on the team has a Service Model. That means everyone on our team can more than just *Think Inc!*—they can actually use the Service Model to assess their job, department, or division. Service Models are everywhere!"

Hal gave a knowing nod.

The Single Cell

The man was curious, "How else can the Service Model can be useful?"

"Sure. Employ it in many situations beyond organizational development. Use it for strategic planning, project management, and task forces. Use it to diagnose problems and prescribe solutions. Use it to write job descriptions and position contracts. Launch a new product or service using it. Have a sales person or a receptionist design his or her job using it. The usefulness of the Service Model is unlimited."

The man posed, "Big organizations are really nothing more than banded together smaller organizations, which are nothing more than clusters of individuals. The whole rests solely on a single building block—one person performing a service. The Service Model gives the power of the whole to the one, and the power of one to the whole."

"Yes," Hal agreed. "The power of being on-purpose is why leaders like Bob Scott and I want team members to be on-purpose business persons. Personal experience with the Service Model helps us more readily relate to the issues of the corporate Service Model. As the power in a single atom is vast, so it is with the potential of one person. Combine the design qualities of the Service Model and the other Pillars—now you're talking nuclear power.

"It makes you appreciate those people in the business who see the big picture and can focus on their job responsibilities."

"Too few are capable of both," the man said.

"Wrong!" Hal corrected. "People are extremely capable. Convey your company Service Model, and they'll surprise you with just how capable they are. Your problem then is staying out of their way."

The man commented, "The Pillars are changing my entire perspective. It's like I've developed a sixth sense of understanding and insight."

"That's as it should be," Hal acknowledged. "In my years of running a business, I observed that discussions have two components: content and process. People process content differently. And each person brings different content to the process.

"The Service Model provides a common process or approach—the same page—to deal with differing content. In times of stress and duress, the only remaining basis for working together may be a common purpose and approach."

The man asked, "It always comes back to purpose, doesn't it?"

"Of course it does."

Hal continued, "You've learned a lot in the past few weeks. Let's reflect for a moment. You've been exposed to a new meaning, mindset, and method to conduct your business. Stepping into the responsibilities of your role will bring a fresh vitality to your work and company. Knowledge without action, however, is nothing. Invest in designing the Service Model with your leadership team, but be sure to invest even more in excellence of execution.

"I appreciate the urgency in your business right now, but there's a mutual friend you need to see. Earlier you mentioned your current mentor, Perry James. Ask him about values as they relate to an on-purpose business, then get back with me. We'll get to Pillar Four then."

"Perry James? How do you two know one another?"

Hal informed, "He's a longtime business colleague."

After leaving Hal, the man tingled with excitement. His basic working knowledge of the Four Pillars was yielding fresh insights and wisdom on several fronts. Once blind to a body of knowledge, he was now gaining sight. How many more people were like him? How many of them were working at his company? As executives?

14
The Value of Values

▼

If there were a controlling power outside the universe...
the only way we could expect it to show itself would be inside
ourselves
as an influence or a command trying to get us to behave
in a certain way.

C. S. Lewis
Mere Christianity

Driving to his lunch meeting to see Perry James, the man admired
the sunny, crisp fall day. He thought, *On such a beautiful day, I'm glad
Perry and I are eating at The Sidewalk Cafe.* Perry is a retired business
executive and owner who served on the boards of several
businesses and nonprofit organizations. He and the man had a
relatively recent, yet meaningful friendship.

Parking his car at the curb next to the cafe, the man saw Perry
seated at an outside table shaded by a large umbrella sipping an
iced tea and reading a magazine. Walking up to greet Perry, his
elder rose and said, "Good to see you my friend. With my travels
the past few months and the arrival of our first grandchild, I've
missed our meetings."

They chatted awhile, and the man admired Perry's pictures of
his granddaughter. Then Perry said, "Congratulations, Mr.
President! A well-deserved honor and great opportunity." In a soft
afterword he added, "I was sad to hear of Fred Taylor's death. Our
paths crossed many times over the years."

"We'll all miss Fred," the man said. He was surprised to learn
that Perry knew Fred.

After placing their lunch orders, the man promptly proceeded to the agenda. "Hal Trudy suggested we talk about values as they relate to the Service Model."

Perry nodded. "Ah, you're finally ready. Values are our internal governors of right and wrong. What else have others told you?"

Recalling his conversation with the Professor, the man added, "Purpose holds it all, even values. Values reside in our throat and gut. Hal explained that values are the nutrients that feed the organization."

"Good," Perry confirmed. "The On-Purpose Principle, this heart-to-heart alignment, transcends even values. It enables people of diverse cultures, races, social circles, or political parties to lay aside differing values to advance a common purpose. Upon this linkage rest the visions, missions, values, and contribution of the organization."

The man observed, "Sounds good on paper. How's it really work?"

"Challenging, always challenging," Perry admitted with a smile. "Yet, try organizing people around values — or anything, for that matter — without a purpose.

"Values are the instilled right and wrong within an organization. These values may or may not, however, be ethical. You know, 'Honor among thieves.' Purpose," Perry stressed, "is always positive, life-giving, and truthful — God's will instead of our will, if you will. Values form the boundary of decision making within which people are free to act."

"Boundaries? Tell me about them," asked the man.

"Boundaries let us know when we cross the border from right to wrong. Without clear boundaries, things go afield. Ill-defined or undefined values limit the ability of an organization to serve and grow. Inevitably, this leads to situational or individual values that are out of context from the whole. They're no longer values, only recommendations...a recipe for disaster.

"Instill values, and you've improved the chances of people having right actions and spirits under pressure. Clear values actually free people to act rather than always being in fear of doing something wrong. One *must* do what's right rather than what's expedient."

"The expedient versus what's right," echoed the man. "I'll remember that. So how do I apply this?"

"Write the values for your business. Violating values is just plain bad business," Perry stated matter-of-factly. "A Service Model without boundaries eventually drifts from its TOP Customers due to poor service. A departure from values signals employees and customers of a drop in value. Employee morale declines and soon the Service Model drifts off-purpose. Profits plummet because the economies and sustainability of the Service Model are lost. All that's left with which to compete is price."

"Pam Dimes said much the same," the man added in recognizing agreement.

Determining Values

The waiter appeared with their lunches. As they ate, Perry pulled a pen from his pocket and drew the Service Model. "The V shape of the model is a reminder that values form the boundary for creating an on-purpose business." With his pen he wrote next to the model the letters A-L-U-E-S, so it would spell VALUES. "Let's explore how values work in the Service Model.

The Service Model

"Values are determined, communicated, checked and engaged, aligned, and, finally, transferred within the Service Model. Let's go through it step by step.

"Step one is values determination. From the point of Purpose at the base of the Service Model comes the Plan. In the Plan, the leader ascertains the values, as well as the vision, missions, and goals.

"Step two is values communication. The values are shared and woven into the fabric of the Plan, People, and Processes. You form the business culture by integrating values into the design and flow of the organization.

"Step three is values checking and engaging. Here we compare the values of the organization with our personal values to check for agreement or conflict. The results are like a traffic signal. Conflicts are red lights that inform us to stop and don't go any further; yellow means proceed with caution; green means go forward. When you advance, this is a decision to engage with and conform to values of the organization.

"Step four is values alignment. This is the integration of the values of the person and the organization. Ideally they're already compatible. Reality mirrors theory when the alignment is high. The Plan, People, Processes, and Performance for serving the customer are aligned. This is personal and corporate integrity.

"Step five is value transfer. This is the front line transaction and relationship-producing value. At this point the entire model has been designed to serve the Customer with the greatest possible value, trust, and benefit.

"There you have it in five easy pieces. Simple, isn't it?"

"I understand, Perry." The man then shared a story. "Recently we changed our health insurance provider largely over a matter of values and trust. Our previous health-care provider questioned, delayed, and negotiated every claim. These repeated actions created distrust. We pay big dollars for medical coverage as an employee benefit. All we got were complaints time and time again. Our people thought we had sold them out.

"Our new health-care provider trusts the patient-doctor relationship to make prudent medical and financial decisions. They see themselves as players, not police, on the health-care team. The premium payment for the new carrier is the same; yet the savings in goodwill and productivity has been incredibly valuable. Trust pays in this case."

"Great example," applauded Perry. "Values *do* influence the customer."

The men finished their meal. Checking his watch, the man anxiously announced, "In five minutes I have to leave for an executive team meeting about our largest customer. Perry, in the short time remaining, please help me determine my values."

"I can't do that," Perry said calmly. "I can only offer you a quick start method so you can work on them some other time. Okay?"

"Deal," the man agreed. He got his pen and paper ready.

"First," Perry began, "write down the names of at least five men and women whom you admire. Next, write down their most admirable personal characteristics. You're making a list, so write freely.

"Next, make another list and record the qualities you most and least admire about yourself. Write next to each of the negative qualities its opposite, or positive, quality. Now you have a list of positive qualities in others and yourself that you admire.

"Pick ten qualities you would like to advance or increase in your life and organization. You now have the raw materials to fashion a set of values. Ta-da!"

"Wow! That's helpful. Thanks!" He handed the waiter his credit card to pay for lunch.

A Confidence

Checking his watch again, the man said, "Perry, I'm sorry, but I have to run as soon as the waiter returns." The man leaned close to Perry, a long-trusted confidant, and quietly divulged, "Confidentially, the business is shaky. The owner and president of GEOMay Company, our largest customer, gave me short notice about meeting. It's about our contract. We're not performing well. Clearly, he's unhappy. Fred has finessed the relationship for years. With Fred gone, we're apt to lose the business if we don't change.

Lots of people could lose their jobs, including me. I'm sick about it. That company has been a major customer for decades. It's almost a sure bet we'll lose their business when the contract expires in six months.

"I've scheduled an emergency executive team meeting to review the account. We're going to work on a new contract with hopes of keeping at least part of the business." The waiter returned the man's charge slip and card. "Pardon me while I dash."

As they shook hands, Perry's departing advice was "Expect the best! Remember to put into practice what you've been learning about leading an on-purpose business."

The man left for his office. Perry's final words rang in his ears. He thought about the upcoming meeting. This was an opportune time to put into practice what he had learned ... on-purpose.

15
The Meeting

▼

Behind every success, there must be a purpose.

Albert E. N. Grey
The Common Denominator of Success

The man anticipated numerous challenges in the executive team meeting. The twenty-five-year relationship with the GEOMay Company was at risk, and so was the company's future.

After opening the meeting, he asked Carter P. Akountz, vice president of finance, to give a financial perspective. Carter reported the facts with an unemotional, detached voice. "GEOMay represents 35 percent of our sales and 30 percent of our net profits. Couple this with their contribution to overhead, and the loss of this account would be devastating."

Sam Cellars, the vice president of sales and marketing, chimed in. "The GEOMay commissions are like base pay for many of my folks. Losing the account will cost me sales and sales reps. My best people will jump ship to competitors. They'll take this relationship and others with them. Try recruiting talented salespeople when your ship is sinking. Do you know how hard that is?

"We need to compete better on price; at least then we might keep a share of the business. Our manufacturing costs are killing us, and our quality control has slid—"

"Hold it there—that's a cheap shot," said Pat Squires, vice president of operations. Pat is a tough, no-nonsense woman with a strong will and a firm grip. "I'm not taking the fall because your sales force can't bring us a correct order form. Do you realize that after all your 'training,' your reps still can't fill out a simple order form? To top it off, they put in change orders daily. Taking such good care of *your* sales persons kills *my* team's efficiencies, *my* performance ratings, and *my* bonus, buster."

"*My* people," Sam defended, "are responding to *our* customers. The customer is always right, and we have to help them."

Cheryl Mann, in addition to being the VP of human resources, is a peacemaker. Having risen through the ranks as a training and development specialist, she could usually be counted on to bring order and harmony. Looking askance at the man she said, "Good luck with this fight. This one's been brewing for ages."

Pat retorted to Sam, "Hey, I'm busting my tail to serve *your* customers. Do you know how many rush jobs I did for your sales team last week alone? Ten! Those disruptions destroy production runs, quality, and budgets. Do I get thanked? No way. From now on your sales guys can just stick it ..."

"STOP! I've heard enough," the man officiated. "This is getting us nowhere. It is like we're having a stupid contest and everyone is winning."

Uncomfortable snickers were followed by silence.

"Let's face it. We're all responsible. If we can't get it right between us, then it's no wonder we can't do right by GEOMay or any customer for that matter. Imagine how our smaller accounts must feel.

"We're in deep trouble. We have a responsibility to tend to here. The stakes are very high for this company, our employees and families, not to mention us as the leaders. Big layoffs or closing the business will rock this work force and community.

"This business will not go belly-up on my watch without a fight. And the fight won't be from within. We're all responsible for this business. Something has to change here and it starts today."

Next, the man directed, "Call your assistants and clear your calendars for the rest of today and tomorrow. Call you families and tell them we're working late tonight. We're not coming out of this room until we have a plan to redesign and rebuild this company with a sound strategy and plan to not just keep the GEOMay contract but to win even more business and grow. We're the leaders, so let's lead! Be back here in 30 minutes."

The executives scurried to their offices to rearrange schedules. The man made his first phone call to Bob Scott. He needed a strategic partner with greater experience in these matters than he had. Fred wouldn't allow outside help, but intellectual isolation hadn't served the company well. Despite this being at a moment's notice, Bob Scott understood the gravity of the matter and showed up.

The Beginning

With their calendars cleared the executives reconvened. Bob Scott was introduced. His role was to provide a measure of On-Purpose advice and insight plus an outside point of view. In matters like this it is rarely a good idea for the leader to facilitate the strategic session so Bob stepped into that role.

Bob asked the man to share what he had recently learned about being an on-purpose business. Their impromptu strategic session had begun. The man explained each Pillar of the on-purpose business. He was determined to get the hearts, heads, and hands of this team aligned to a single unifying purpose.

"Why does this company exist?" he asked.

They came up with twenty-four reasons. At Bob's suggestion, they used the tennis tournament method to bracket and advance to the most meaningful purpose of the organization. It read, "Our company exists to serve by Shedding Light."

"Shedding Light" carried meaningful nuances. It meant illuminating darkness and dispelling confusion. It meant to be a source for solutions rather than greater doubt. Their purpose meant they could shed or lighten the load for each other, employees, and customers by working together to make things and situations right and more manageable. Implied was a sense of shining and sharing joy and good cheer, as well as offering an adaptability and flexibility that enabled them to serve in a variety of ways. Previously, they reported information with one another but they had never had a high standard of transparency and interactivity with the information to make it meaningful and useful.

Next, Bob encouraged them to write a unifying company vision. Pat Squires recalled the image of an old-time lamplighter. In the days before electric streetlights, lamplighters would walk the streets lighting gas lampposts. Their service brought safety, security, and commerce to unlit areas. Street lamps offered a constant presence to guide, direct, and warn. They would become a modern day lamplighter in their industry.

The purpose and vision of the company would be lived through the following missions:

1. Development of People
2. Communications
3. Products and Services

They wrote several values that they considered essential to integrity. The first was, *Truth sets us free.* Fred was skilled at parsing the truth in such a way they he wasn't lying but he was cleverly deceiving. Shedding light dictated that dealing truthfully created better relationships and results more quickly and peacefully.

The second value was, *Be real.* Company politics, posturing, and "politeness" kept people fake. This culture of phoniness created cover-your-rear-end actions, deceit, sabotage, and non-acceptance. To be real meant to be forthright and honest in all dealings.

A third value was, *Context matters.* It was easy live in a silo and ignore the problems of others, but this was a counter-productive approach to progress. One couldn't shed responsibility by saying, "That's not my job," once they understood that their life and work had a context that affects other people. This extended beyond the company to citizenship. They had held jobs, but hadn't realized their work to be part of a calling of greater contribution and good with and on so many lives.

For each value they wrote a simple statement and then expanded it into the reality of their culture. Honest conversation about what they liked and disliked about their working relationship and environment provided the fodder to craft their core values.

Bob next asked each person to share what excited him or her personally about Shedding Light. This was a first pass at establishing the On-Purpose Principle—linking personal purpose with the organizational purpose.

They tapped into the Tingle factor. The business had awesome potential. In this conversation a transformation began. It was a feeling of being more like the founders of the business instead of the curators as they had been. The opportunity to serve all the stakeholders—the community, customers, shareholders, employees, and themselves—was in their hands.

This highly charged session was productive. With renewed energy and cohesiveness, they had lightened their agenda by focusing on the vital few essentials rather than the diffusing many distractions. They had established a purpose and simple plan for the business. By borrowing from the best of the past and the present, they had designed a promising future.

The evening grew late. Bob recommended an adjournment and asked the man to close with his final thoughts on the day. Here the man made a bold move that even surprised Bob.

The man stood silently and thoughtfully before his C-suite executives. They could tell he was searching his mind for the right words. After a minute, he addressed them. Scanning the room and, in turn, looking each member in the eye, he said, "Thanks for the greatest days of my career and for all your hard work. In a few short hours, we've re-created this company. Now I have one final request. I want job resignations from all of you."

Their mouths dropped open in utter disbelief. He motioned with an open hand for them to stop and listen. "I have a proposition for you. Tomorrow morning at eight, I'm rehiring, but I have to know where each of you stands with this new company. If this isn't right for you, then I will accept your resignation with no prejudice whatsoever.

"I promise you'll receive outplacement and a continuation of your salary and benefits for up to a year or until you land another job. On the other hand, if this new venture excites you, then be here tomorrow morning at eight. From then on, 100 percent of your focus and commitment is required. You're either in or out. No more discussions tonight. We'll reconvene at eight a.m. Now get out of here. Go home and sleep on this. I'll clean up here."

They adjourned at 9:30 p.m.

Day One

As the man stayed behind to clean up pizza boxes from dinner, he reflected with Bob on the events of the day. In the beginning, each person had a different understanding of the purpose of the business. At one point Pat Squires had observed, "It's no wonder we're always at odds. We've never been this honest with each other. We've never shared a common purpose. I didn't really understand the big picture of business, let alone this business, before today. We're in bad shape."

Bob recalled Carter's admission, "After thirty-plus years as being 'just a numbers guy,' the on-purpose business method opened my eyes. I've honored my profession, but I was comfortably blind to my greater responsibilities as a business person and leader. I'm sorry, team. No more! Let's take it to the next level."

Congratulating the man, Bob said, "That was a bold and ingenious move firing everyone. Your executive team accomplished more in a day than they had in decades. Most important of all, a spirit of optimism binds them together as never before. I'm proud of the way you conducted yourself."

"Bob, thanks for being here at a moment's notice and then being here long into the night. You're my on-purpose partner and I couldn't have done this without you. I know you can't be here tomorrow. I'm confident, however, that our working session will go well … assuming I still have a team that is!"

Tomorrow, the matter at hand was the GEOMay relationship and contract with this "new company." Shoving the pizza boxes into a large trashcan the man shut off the lights. They headed to their cars. The man stood at Bob's car door as the engine roared to life. Bob lowered his car window and said, "I wonder who's showing up tomorrow morning." He winked and drove off into the darkness leaving the man standing there to ponder.

16
Starting Over

▼

Men and women should cooperate to study and solve their
problems
without envy or personal ambition and
find their reward in a handsome aggregate result
in which their touch can be felt
but from which their grasp is absent.

Newton Baker (1871–1937)
U.S. Secretary of War under President Woodrow Wilson

The entire leadership team arrived at the office early. Excited to
make progress, the meeting began at 7:30 a.m., thirty minutes
early. Without exception, each person applied for a "new job."
With *their* on-purpose business still in creation, the team eagerly
anticipated the challenges of the GEOMay Company relationship.
A positive energy charged the room.

The man smiled and spoke, "I'm so encouraged by your
response. Yesterday, for the first time, I felt like I really got to know
each of you. I found out what excites, engages, and matters to you.
Let's be a phoenix rising from our ashes." Heads nodded around
the room.

The man posed the purpose question, "How can we serve
GEOMay by 'shedding light'?"

Sam said, "Last night my head was spinning with ideas and
answers to problems that have dogged us for years. With a few
marketing enhancements we can position ourselves to rocket into
industry leadership once again. Greatness remains in this business.
Before yesterday, no one wanted to hear ideas let alone work with

me to enrich them." Sam was a salesman at heart. It was understandable that he talked with such enthusiasm.

The surprise was Carter, old Mr. Steady. He worked at the company for well over twenty years. Prior to that, he had been with a public accounting firm. This morning Carter's typically monotone voice bubbled. "About four this morning, I was lying in bed wide awake … thinking, actually thinking about the business. We've been in a rut for so long, I had forgotten how to think. That *Think Inc!* jolted me — oxygen to my brain.

"Do you know that our pricing model hasn't changed in years? Such a dated approach disadvantages us. I came in very early this morning to reread the details of the GEOMay contract. There's an incentive bonus we've never met and penalties we rarely miss. I've come up with a way we can offer very competitive pricing for GEOMay that can actually save us some costs, ease the wide swings in sales, and enable us to earn the incentive bonus. I need everyone's input, however, to make sure this is doable.

"Done right it will create a more manageable flow in Pat's operations. The disruptive special handling on orders can be minimized. That will keep Pat's costs from spiraling out of her control and get her budget in line."

Cheryl contributed, "Those aren't Pat's costs and budget. They're *ours*! We all own them." Each person nodded in agreement.

Pat added, "I love it! Carter, let's explore your ideas right away." Then, turning to Sam, Pat continued, "Actually, Sam, I thought we might work together to create a more competitive package for our customers and especially the GEOMay Company. We'll use the Service Model. There are incredibly talented and innovative people working with me. True lamplighters, if you know what I mean." She turned and winked at the man. "Sam, involve us earlier in the sales process, and we can work miracles if given half a chance." Sam smiled in delight.

Cheryl offered, "I'll pull together a series of short training programs over the next few days to bring others up to speed on the Pillars of the on-purpose business. Let's record an introductory video of our purpose, plan, and values so we can do desktop introduction prior to the stand-up training. We can spread the excitement throughout the company. Hey, coach," she said, looking at the man, "give me an hour to interview and tape you for this program." The man said, "Interview the entire executive team." All agreed that was an even better approach.

The man watched in stunned wonder. By unleashing the power of being on-purpose and releasing his once closely held burden of "business ownership," his C-suite executives embraced the challenges with personal and team vigor. Petty defenses of respective corporate turf gave way to the greater cause. The light switch of being on-purpose was definitely turned on. Each person shed light on aspects of the business that had been tightly hidden in dark information silos for too many years. Each team member was thinking as a business person instead of a narrow-minded functional specialist. It was unlike anything he had experienced under The Old Man's watch.

The balance of the morning was invested in hammering out a Service Model approach for GEOMay. If the GEOMay contract was practically lost anyway, then they had everything to gain. By acknowledging their obvious weaknesses they could address them, focus on their strengths, and play with abandon.

Over the next week they hammered out a new proposal in anticipation of the meeting with George F. May III, grandson of the founder of GEOMay Company. The company was coming alive with being on-purpose. Creative energy and attitudes energized everyone. With Cheryl's help, the video and training sessions on the Pillars were a hit! They named the cross-company training series TOP Performer, short for The On-Purpose Performer. On-Purpose was buzzing in the hallways, desktops, and workbenches. The purpose, vision, missions, and values statements guided the team with clarity and resolve. Individual confidence and mutual trust grew with each passing day. Corporate renewal followed on the heels of personal transformations. The Tingle was electrifying.

The Moment of Truth

The day of the GEOMay meeting was finally here. In advance of the meeting the man got George's consent to give the team thirty minutes for a presentation. He said he would politely listen, although his agenda was to inform.

A dignified George F. May III and several key executives arrived. The presentation followed a simple five-step "shedding light" process. First, the man and his team did the unthinkable in business. They admitted their known mistakes, asked for forgiveness for their poor performance, and accepted full responsibility. Next, they shed light on the problems as best they could from GEOMay's perspective. Then they shared the fundamental transformation from becoming an on-purpose business. Step four was to provide a schedule for implementing the new changes. Step five was a written promise to perform, signed by every member of the executive team, supervisor, and rank and file of the business. It all made a dramatic impression on George.

At this point in the presentation, the man made a bold move. Holding up the existing contract, he stated, "Almost six months remain on this contract. George, we've worked together a long time, and you know I'm a man of my word. Here's the deal. I'll tear up this contract right now if you want. We'll end it right here and now with no strings attached. Of course, we'll carry you through until you shift to another vendor. For all intents and purposes, the contract in my hand is with a company that no longer exists so it is all but null and void.

"Ours is a new company," the man declared proudly. He panned his hand toward the vice presidents as the symbols of a new company. He looked George directly in the eye and said, "We want a new contract with GEOMay Company. Our company is about 'Shedding Light.' We've prepared a new contract, and with your permission let's forge a fresh relationship between our companies. May I review it with you?"

George cautiously said, "Proceed."

The team laid out the Service Model designed just for GEOMay. It was revolutionary in the industry: faster deliveries, a tiered pricing schedule, and a dedicated "concierge" customer service program with individual assignments to specific people in GEOMay.

George, however, had his doubts. "Why should I believe you can do this after the years of falling performance you've just admitted?"

The man responded, "George, there's only one reason. The men and women in this room and in this company give you our word. We'll perform as promised. We're so confident we can perform on this contract that I'll add a handwritten addendum. With a thirty-day written notice, we're gone. It's that easy. We want you raving about us rather than raging at us.

"Successful pilot programs are underway right now. Glitches are bound to happen; yet we're committed to learning and improving over the remaining six months on the old contract."

Moving from the defensive to the offensive, the man asked the question. "So, George, do I tear up this old contract? Do you walk or do you stay to redefine a new, improved relationship? We want to be a lamplighter for your company. What's your decision?"

The moment of truth arrived. The man felt the tension, yet he remained confident. He knew this proposed contract would be hard for George to decline. Also, he knew his company and people were on the verge of a breakthrough. If George wouldn't buy it, then others would. The GEOMay contract enabled an orderly progression to the changeover. In that regard it was important.

George was jotting notes. Without raising his head, he peered over his Ben Franklin half-framed glasses and coldly stated, "My grandfather taught me to shoot straight with people. That's what I'm doing. After all, you employ many people in this community and others; families depend on you for a paycheck. So out of respect for the years we've worked together ... I'm here to inform you ahead of time that we will not be renewing the current contract. I wanted you to be warned so you could begin making alternative arrangements. Today, I end doing business with this company. You offered me an out and I'm taking it. Tear up that contract."

The man felt his heart sink. The other team members gasped. Had they miscalculated the damage? Apparently.

Had the man been a fool to think they could salvage this relationship? If George couldn't see the logic and strength of this proposal, would others? Was bankruptcy protection their last alternative? The reality of losing the GEOMay account hit hard.

Having invested so much of himself the past week in the possibilities of success, he hadn't prepared himself for a different outcome. With George and everyone else watching, he began tearing up the contract. With each shred, he hardened his resolve to excel.

George dispassionately watched the ritual death of the relationship. When the man finished, George broke the dead silence. "I wondered if you really would tear up that contract."

George's countenance changed. A smile broke from the corner of his mouth. "I'm fascinated with the thirty minutes of magic you all have presented. You took my reasons for terminating this contract and addressed them all. It's like you read my mind. In fact, you exceeded what I thought was possible. You've shown genuine creativity I didn't think existed in this company, or industry for that matter. I'm impressed.

"I'll engage your *new* company. Take the six months remaining under the old contract to get your act together. Deliver as promised, and I'll renew. If you don't make it right — we're gone. You've been warned. Do we have an understanding?"

"Yes! We *will* perform," the man pledged. His spirits soared and around the room his teammates' faces shone with pride.

George continued, "I like the leadership and fresh thinking you're providing since Fred's retirement and passing. There's a strong and positive attitude here. I foresee a bright future ... assuming you perform as promised."

Now looking at the man, George added, "I'm imposing one condition. You proposed a stronger alliance between our businesses. I agree. Let's get our people working together as soon as possible. Our people need to be a part of putting together that, uh ... Service Model, I think you called it." Then turning to one of the executives accompanying him, George said, "Let's work with these good people to partner in their success. I sense we'll all be better off together."

George stood and shook hands with the man, Cheryl, Carter, Sam, and Pat. After George's departure, the team gave each other high fives and hugs to celebrate. They had averted an imminent disaster. More importantly, their first on-purpose proposal was triumphant.

Massive work lay ahead. Yet, they could proceed with newfound confidence in a purpose, plan, people, process, and performance aligned to serve their customers. They tingled at the possibilities.

For the first time, they had done a major deal without The Old Man. This was their deal. The man felt great about the company and the new milestone. He wondered to himself, *Now, how in the world do we sustain this? I've never done anything like this before. This is why Pillar Four, the Manner of the on-purpose business, is important.*

The time was right to see Hal again. In the midst of his largest career victory, he knew he was still short one Pillar — the Manner. What more could there be?

17
The On-Purpose Palette

▼

Today, systems thinking is needed more than ever
because we are becoming overwhelmed by complexity....
Organizations break down, despite individual brilliance and
innovative products,
because they are unable to pull their diverse functions and talents
into a productive whole.

Peter M. Senge
The Fifth Discipline

Finding his way to the familiar park bench, the man sat and waited for Hal. He appeared on a path carrying a shovel and an empty watering can.

The men shook hands. Hal welcomed the man: "Good to see you. I brought my shovel in case that little stick fails to garner your attention anymore," Hal teased. "I was delighted when you called to share your victory."

"Hal, it's remarkable." The man recounted the story of the GEOMay contract. Smiling from ear to ear, Hal listened to the man's command performance. "The three Pillars we've used so far are awesome. We devised a memory jogger to help use the Pillars. We call it the On-Purpose Palette."

"Tell me about it," Hal requested.

"Artists use a palette to hold and mix colors so they can create what they want. That's what the Palette does for us. Each Pillar is assigned a primary color. The On-Purpose Principle is red for the heart. *Think Inc!* we labeled blue because it deals with the mind's eye and blue-sky thinking. The Service Model is the yellow Pillar because we use it day-to-day. Just as the yellow sun rises and sets daily so too does our daily work."

Hal's eyes twinkled. "I love it! Go on."

The man offered, "By mixing the three primary colors of red, blue, and yellow, any color can be created. We see challenges or opportunities as having three perspectives. Once each perspective is discussed, we mix the colors to fit the picture. This enables us to deal systematically with the full spectrum of issues."

"For example?" Hal invited.

"For example ..."—the man was thinking—"to increase sales. What's the challenge? Before the Palette, we would try promotions, advertising, sales incentives, and so forth. They're all short-term performance enhancers but not necessarily connected to a long-term approach. We now take a systematic way to approach a sales increase. Here's how we assess and correct our problems.

"RED: Using the On-Purpose Principle, we evaluate sales from a personal and organizational perspective. *On the organizational side*: Have we clearly articulated the purpose of the organization so the sales team can meaningfully align with it? They have to believe in what they and we are doing. Are we drifting off-purpose? Are Technical and Tingle aligning for top performance? *On the personal side*: Do people feel a sense of belonging and personal importance? Is a sales person's purpose aligned with the purpose of the organization? In other words, is the Tingle high or low? Is Technical training needed?"

Hal nodded his head. "Insights to the right answers are often found in the right questions."

"Now, there's the truth," the man corroborated.

"BLUE: With *Think Inc!*" the man continued, "we evaluate our mindset relative to sales. Are we thinking like owners and presidents? Have we considered long- and short-term effects? Do we understand the profit-and-loss potential? Are responsibility and authority connected? What are the personal, professional, and corporate risks and rewards? Are they appropriate for the people involved? Has some Stink Inc. or blaming crept into our midst?

"YELLOW: the Service Model. Have we researched and thought through the customer chain? What needs to improve at the front line? What are our customers saying? Do we have structural problems within the Service Model? Are the linkages and relative order from level to level properly aligned? Have we changed the Plan yet not put in motion the appropriate changes at the Performance level and the levels in between? Have we made an inadvertent change at the Performance level that isn't supported by the lower levels or vice versa? Are we communicating effectively? Have we altered or departed from our values?

"Using the Palette, we are a company of business people. From the mail room to the board room, everyone is engaged in learning and improving the business because it's as easy as remembering the three primary colors that we learned in kindergarten."

Hal commented, "The palette is vividly ingenious. With all those on-purpose business persons, I predict great things for your business. Well done!"

"Thanks. I'm ready to move on to Pillar Four: 'Doing More of What You Do Best More Profitably.' Will you help?" asked the man.

Hal nodded and then posed a question. "Using your Palette, what color is Pillar Four?"

The man snapped his head back. "I don't know."

"Remember that the Manner of the on-purpose business embodies the other Pillars. May I suggest white as the color for Pillar Four? If you shine a white light through a prism, a rainbow emerges. White light holds it all."

"Hal," the man said, "that's a natural phenomena! I love it. Thanks for 'shedding light' on that."

"Consider it my contribution. I see lots of rainbows when I'm spraying water in the sunlight. Now, let's get you to your next on-purpose partner. See John Harold. I believe you know each other?"

"Yes, we do," said the man, hiding a grimace. He thought, *Of all the people, why John Harold?* John was the senior pastor of a church. *What can a pastor know about building a business? Becoming an on-purpose business sure stretches my comfort zone.*

Hal closed with, "Our lessons are complete. We'll visit again, though."

The man added his appreciation. "Thanks for mentoring me. One last thing: I'm glad you didn't need that shovel today!" With that, Hal snatched up the shovel and faked a strike. The two men laughed and shared a parting hug.

18
Pillar Four:
Matters of Manner

▼

Simple, clear purpose and principles give rise to complex and
intelligent behavior.
Complex rules and regulations give rise to simple and stupid
behavior.

Dee Hock
Founder and CEO Emeritus of Visa International
Author, *The Chaordic Organization*

It was late in the afternoon as the man headed to the church office
to meet John Harold. Passing by the sanctuary door, he heard
music. Peering inside he discovered it was a children's choir
practicing. Their voices carried an angelic and peaceful sound.
Now standing by the open door, he listened and breathed in the
music. The purity of this drew him into a calm reflection of the
remarkable and recent changes in his life. He was grateful for his
life.

Turning from the door, his thoughts shifted to his upcoming
appointment. What this meeting had to do with his business, he didn't
know. He thought, *I'm a businessman, a pragmatist, someone who needs proof.
As far as I know, the whole world is just one big accident that keeps fermenting like
witches' brew.* Matters of faith unsettled him because they seemed so
contrary to the world about him.

The man and Pastor John Harold were acquainted from a
previous visit. John invited him to consider spiritual matters more

seriously. The man wasn't looking forward to this meeting because he hadn't.

"Faith," he would say to his wife, "is a personal matter. I'm a good person. That's what really counts." And then he would think of questions like *Does God exist? How good is good enough? Why am I here?* It was confusing and, he decided, better left alone.

Stepping inside the church office, the man spied John Harold near the receptionist's desk. At their prior meeting, John had worn a madras shirt without a clerical collar. He had humorously described himself as being "undercover." Today, he wore a black shirt with a white clerical collar.

The man joked, "I see you're in battle dress today! Are you going to 'save' me? Maybe I should come back when it's safe."

The pastor smiled. "Stay! Salvation is already a done deal when you're ready. Today, perhaps?"

The man cowered in mock fear.

Undaunted, the minister invited, "Stay anyway. Otherwise, how will you learn about Pillar Four?"

"Deal! Now you're talking," the businessman replied. "The Manner. That's why I'm here."

John, pretending to strike an auctioneer's gavel, said, "Sold on Pillar Four!" Then placing his left arm around the man's shoulder, John chuckled, "You asked for that." The man agreed.

"Let's go to my office and talk about the Manner of the on-purpose church — oops, I mean the on-purpose business. Same Manner, just a different setting."

Now seated on comfortable chairs in the pastor's office, John commented, "Pillar Four saved me from major burnout. I learned to let go of what I don't do best and leave it to someone else who does do it best. Being on-purpose is freeing and fun.

"Many of my peers try to do it all and be 'perfect' instead of being themselves. The diverse challenges of leading, let alone serving in a church, can result in clergy burnout or worse. Our personal setbacks have private consequences. Plus they can be so public that we hinder the very cause and person we're advancing. Being on-purpose is vital for maintaining a grounded and healthy life perspective, especially for leaders within the fish bowl of the public eye."

"Sounds a lot like my job as president of the company," the man said. "My waking hours are consumed with work. I guess being a pastor *is* like running a business."

John nodded in agreement. "That's why we must be true to our purpose. It's easy to become seduced by our public. Pillar Four helps us be at peace and focused on who we are and aren't. Then we act accordingly."

"Great," the man said with enthusiasm. "Why is Pillar Four known as the Manner?"

"There are several reasons," John explained. "Manners are learned choices and conduct. It takes effort to exercise good manners. Good manners elevate us from a natural way into a more refined state. Pillar Four is all about choosing to act, think, behave, and organize more consistently by 'Doing More of What You Do Best More Profitably' personally and professionally."

"You slipped in some new stuff: 'personally and professionally.' What's up with this?"

"The church is not the building, it's the people," John explained. Moving to the edge of his chair, he added, "The same is true of any business or organization. As the people grow, so grows the organization. We leaders must be growing because our influence touches the entire organization.

"Let's put it in terms of a family. A well-mannered father will likely pass gracious manners to his children. Mastery of manners is an important life attribute. Manners may appear as niceties for polite society, however, they're truly based in practicalities."

"Manners matter," the man agreed. "Manners are also 100 percent my choice, once I have awareness. There are very few other places in business or life where I can say that."

"Yes," John confirmed. "If we lack a manner upon which to direct our lives or business, then by which manner are we running it?"

"Without a chosen manner, I guess I choose whatever seems right at the time," ventured the man.

"And the consequences of situational rather than systematic conduct is ...?" John led him.

"Chaos. Confusion. Haphazardness. No consistency. I'm here; I'm there. One day it's this decision; the next day it's another. As the leader my confusion gets amplified through the organization."

"Absolutely," John agreed. "Manners simplify living and life. They help integrate, synthesize, and align a person's heart, head, and hands within their values. It's the same for an organization. A manner is a rule of life that helps you stay on-purpose in your new way of life or work."

"I don't get it," the man commented.

"I realize the Bible isn't a reference in your life," John said, pausing to smile before he continued, "and yet, there's a short story from the Bible that clearly illustrates the point. May I tell you a Bible story?"

"Hey, I'm here to learn," the man replied. "Go ahead, use whatever book you want if it helps me learn to be a better leader."

19
The Great Manner

▼

I love being on-purpose. I'm saying no to increasingly better opportunities
and saying yes more frequently to the best opportunities.

Paul G. Anthes
President, Financial Advisory Corporation

The man didn't know that John Harold was once the chief financial officer (CFO) of a successful privately owned company. Following a call into the ministry in his late thirties, he changed careers. He related especially well to business people and their day-to-day challenges, pressures, and temptations because he was once in the thick of the business world.

"So tell me the Bible story," invited the man, "so I can understand this Manner stuff."

John smiled and thought, *He's just like I was — all business. Get the deal done; do the transaction and move on to the next. Avoid getting too deep.*

John began, "You'll need some background to appreciate the story. Have you heard of the Ten Commandments?"

"Heard of them, of course," the man replied. "I even saw the movie."

"Good," said the pastor. "Now let me set a later scene. One day, more than a thousand years after Moses brought the commandments down from the mountain, the chief priests and Pharisees were questioning Jesus about His teaching 'credentials.' These powerful men were the keepers of the Jewish law, rules, and traditions. Jesus' radical teachings had threatened their leadership, authority, position, and power. So the Pharisees set a trap, hoping to entangle Jesus with His own words.

"One of the Pharisees, a lawyer and religious scholar, set an ambush by asking Jesus, 'Teacher, which is the greatest commandment in the Law?'"

The man asked, "How's that a trick question?"

"Look at Jesus' three possible responses," the pastor explained. "He could have given no response, or chosen one of the commandments, or responded that all the laws are equal.

"The entrapment was this: The 'correct' response, according to the Pharisees, was that all commandments were from God through Moses, and therefore all are equal. If Jesus answered this way, He would show that He was a traditionalist and under their authority. They could then readily denounce His other teachings.

"If Jesus responded that one law was above the others, He would be deemed a heretic, and His blasphemy would be a punishable offense.

"Finally, if He chose not to respond, He would be deemed a novice with no knowledge or authority in the Law."

Listening intently, the man said, "Fascinating—more like prime-time TV than the Bible." A thought flashed in his mind: *Can this ancient story actually be relevant to today?* Now up on the edge of his chair, he demanded, "So, what was His answer?"

John Harold paused, then said, "Jesus replied, 'Love the Lord your God with all your heart and with all your soul and with all your mind. This is the first and greatest commandment. And the second is like it: Love your neighbor as yourself. All the Law and the Prophets hang on these two commandments.'"

"Bold choice," said the man with admiration. "He took the heretic response. A guy with guts. How'd our boys the Pharisees take it?"

"As you might expect," John replied, "most branded Him a heretic; a few were convicted by the truth. That's the irony. The Pharisees were so intent on the letter of the law that they were blind to Christ's profound message of the spirit of the law being grounded in love, not rules. He distilled complex and even seemingly contradictory teachings, laws, traditions, rules, and customs into a simple *manner* of conduct. In doing so, He reformed their faith. His brilliant response is known as the Great Commandment."

"Inspiring story! Is that really in the Bible?" the man questioned. "Or did you make that up for me?"

John laughed. "Look at the book of Matthew in the twenty-second chapter, verses thirty-four to forty. By the way, that's in the New Testament, the books way toward the back," he teased. "You'll find many profound and practical truths in the Bible that apply to life and business. Read it sometime."

Amused by the man's raw skepticism, the pastor commented, "You are so much like I was years ago. It's amazing." He shared some of his business background.

The man asked, "Why do you say we're alike?"

"Your apprehension of the Bible and organized religion is how I felt. I had all these preconceived notions on faith, God, Jesus, and other spiritual matters. Religion was a poisonous and divisive topic so I avoided it and went about my business.

"I understand that your agenda today is Pillar Four. Promise me, however, that one day soon we'll get together man-to-man to talk about the spiritual foundation of life." Sliding into his old business terminology, the on-purpose pastor extended his hand. "Deal?"

"You're good," said the man, accepting John's hand. "If you hadn't said you were a CFO, I would have guessed you to be the VP of sales and marketing. I'll shake on it and listen to your pitch someday.

"Today, let's get back to the Manner, please."

The Great Commandment

"We already are," John replied. "The Manner is a simplifying operational mantra that equips us to right ourselves regardless of the situation, dilemma, or conflict. Through the Great Commandment, Jesus was shedding light on all the teachings, laws, traditions, rules, and customs, especially the Ten Commandments. In essence, if you live according to this one manner, everything else will take care of itself."

The man's ears perked up. He stopped John and said, "You said 'shedding light.' That's the purpose statement for my company. Amazing that you would use those words."

The pastor responded, "What's even more remarkable is Jesus said, 'I am the "Light" of the world.' Are you aware that your purpose statement has strong spiritual implications?"

The man rolled his eyes, crossed his arms, and squirmed in his chair, "Gimme a break. Tell me about the Manner."

John knowingly chuckled to himself at the irony of the man wanting to shed light but he just couldn't handle that much "wattage" at this dawning. Respectfully, he continued meeting the man where he was in his quest, "The Manner of an on-purpose business is 'Doing More of What You Do Best More Profitably.' Let's diagram it into three parts.

"Let's start with the center third, 'What You Do Best.' When you're on-purpose, you're operating in your best self. Excellence is internally set. When you're in your best place, then meaning, fulfillment, and performance are more able to follow."

The man nodded his understanding.

John resumed, "The lead third, 'Doing More,' relates to the Service Model, or Pillar Three. Using the Service Model we can make 'what we do best' happen with greater regularity and consistency.

"The final third of the statement is 'More Profitably.' I'm using *profit* to mean 'contribution' or adding value in its broadest sense. Contribution is both a financial term and a term of generosity. Profit is positive difference making in both the financial and the social context.

"Social profit exists in smiles, hugs, happiness, trust, and positive feelings. Financial profit is the excess of revenues after expenses and is one of many measures rather than the only measure of profit. Get that distinction! We business types tend to lock in on financial profit exclusively. Recall that the Service Model is designed to create value at the front line."

The man smiled. "I like it. 'Doing More of What You Do Best More Profitably' is a method to success that elegantly integrates both the social and the financial aspects that create an on-purpose business. I've watched our business try to do more of what we *don't* do best, only to end up unprofitable — in terms of morale and finances. It's disastrous."

The pastor added, "What you've just described is the malady menacing lots of leaders. We try to be all things to all people so we over diversify when, in fact, we're just diluting our purpose.

"In the church our work is called, 'ministry.' Serving is never-ending, because the needs are. So where does one draw the line? At this church, we believe in the whole body of Christ at work, and we are but one member of the larger body. We focus on our unique purpose and contribution while referring many needs to other churches and ministries. Businesses must likewise resist the temptation of trying to be all things to all customers, yet care for those who find their way to the door."

Provided, Receiving, Giving

"I'm curious about something," said the man. "What's the purpose statement for this church?"

"'Revealing Truth.' The longer version is 'To the glory of God, we exist to serve by Revealing Truth.'"

"What is the truth you're revealing?" the man inquired.

"Since you asked," said John with a smile, "each word in our purpose statement packs a punch. 'Revealing' means demonstrating, showing, leading, and giving. 'Truth' is a standard of being factual, forthright, honest, and accurate. Jesus describes himself as Truth. We believe that the only Truth is that which comes from God directly or indirectly. The Bible holds Truth. God reveals Himself to us every day if we'll look and are willing to have it revealed. In turn, we're to encourage others to look for the revelation of truth from God, within themselves, and with others.

"Positioning ourselves by our manner, 'Revealing Truth' is a miraculous gift we're being provided, receiving, and giving in potentially every instance of our lives."

"And you believe that?" asked the man. "Give me an example."

"Let's take our relationship," John stated. "I reveal truth to you when I share the manner of an on-purpose business or if I invite you to deepen your spiritual perspective." John scratched his head. "Funny thing is, you listen to me about the truth in business matters, but not about what I do best ... God. Odd, isn't it?"

The man shrugged his shoulders and teased, "Hey, you can lead a horse to water, but you can't make him drink — right? Anyway, you've been terrific thus far. I hate to ruin a friendship by discussing religion."

"You're persistent in your resistance," laughed the pastor.

"Sorry," the man apologized. "It's just that religion isn't really for me."

"Me either," John agreed.

"Hey, that's your specialty — what you do best," protested the man.

John chuckled and calmly replied, "My specialty is 'Revealing Truth,' not 'shoving truth.'" The journey you're on is all too familiar."

"Where am I?" prompted the man.

"You're close."

"Close to where?" questioned the man.

John reassured, "Close to being on-purpose, of course. You've already had lots of revelation. Still, you're in the earlier stages of the On-Purpose Process. Being on-purpose has even greater usefulness and depth. You've been on a search for revelation because you have a pressing need. Eventually, curiosity will get you exploring the greater depth found in the spiritual aspects of your work ... and life."

"Why do you say that about me?" questioned the man.

"Your search today is of a work nature. Work is a gift from God granted in the Garden of Eden. The interplay of the secular and the sacred has always been at work. In this light, business is a platform designed to reveal the deeper need. Your life has a built-in design. And you have a free will to accept or reject it. In the church we talk of being in God's will. In laypeople's language that's being on-purpose. Remember the light switch? You're either off- or on-purpose ... out of or in God's will.

"Embracing one's divine design rather than fleeing it, invites God to work in your life. As a business person you need to be forewarned about God. He's got serious resources," joked the pastor. "Plus He forgives debts!"

The man laughed nervously at the paradoxical nature of this conversation. His head was spinning. Pastor John's words disturbed yet comforted him. The man resisted this line of conversation, yet he had invited it. He came to talk business, yet his spiritual life was involved. Right now he could only manage just so much new thinking.

He brought the discussion back within his comfort zone, "Great. But how do I apply the Manner to my business?"

"As the leader of the company goes, so goes the business. Your best and worst attributes are amplified throughout the organization. Your position, like mine, carries high visibility and responsibility. There's no escaping your personal influence on the health and well-being of the organizations you lead, whether it's a business, church, or family.

"Also the more aware you are of the Manner, the more you're able to see and advise your team members. As the leader you need additional insight beyond technical performance."

"This comes back to aligning one's heart, head, and hands within one's values, doesn't it?"

"Yes! Let's tie it all together." John borrowed the man's

PILLAR FOUR: THE MANNER

Doing More of ...	What You Do Best	More Profitably
Hands	Heart	Head
Pillar Three	Pillar One	Pillar Two
Service Model	The On-Purpose Principle	Think Inc!
Yellow	Red	Blue

journal and sketched out a table. "Take a look."

The man looked at the chart and added the Palette colors. He briefly explained the Palette to the pastor. The man commented, "The Manner really is like the Great Commandment. The first three Pillars are contained in the Manner."

"You've got it! Now live it!" John exclaimed with a smile.

Awesome Responsibility

Their time together had been brief, yet the pastor's touch was indelibly imprinted on the man. Walking to his car, he contemplated, *No matter where I turn, the influence of my purpose on the lives of others keeps arising. John was right; I can't avoid it. I never sensed the high leverage my purpose has on the ultimate performance of the organization. It's an awesome responsibility.*

Turning the key in the ignition, he cranked up his car and pulled out of the church parking lot. As he did, his cell phone rang into his car's sound system. He answered, "Hello."

"Hi! Jackie said I might catch you in your car," said a familiar voice.

"Hi, Professor! Great to hear from you! So what's the purpose of your call?" asked the man, laughing at turning around the Professor's usual question to him.

"I've created a monster," joked the Professor. "Bob Scott and I talked. We've arranged for you to meet Wayne Bell tomorrow morning at eight. Jackie rearranged some morning meetings so you're free to meet while he's in town. He travels a lot so we squeezed in the meeting.

"Pardon my boldness with your schedule. This is important. Wayne leaves for the coast on a business trip in two days. Before he leaves, you two need to meet. By the way, dress comfortably."

"I'll be there." The man plugged Wayne's address into his smartphone for the next day's trip.

Pulling into his driveway, the man's arrival was met with excitement from his kids at the front window. As the kids poured out of the house to greet their father's unusually early arrival from work, he thought, *Wow, work isn't the only place where I need to be on-purpose. I hope I'm an on-purpose parent.*

With the swarm of his kids, he walked into his home and gave his wife a warm hug and kiss on the cheek. After dinner and the kids' bedtime, he crashed onto the couch and fell asleep. His wife awoke him to come to bed. It was a few minutes before eleven p.m.

The events of the past few weeks had been exhilaratingly exhausting. As the eleventh hour with GEOMay approached, he wondered what the future would hold.

20
The Solo Owner

▼

I have seen the business that God has given to everyone to be busy
with....
It is God's gift that all should eat and drink and take pleasure in all
their toil.

Ecclesiastes 3:10,13, NRSV

The man awoke feeling refreshed. He threw on casual clothes and
grabbed a quick breakfast. Jeans and a sweater were a welcome
change from his usual Tom James suit, polished leather shoes, and
Windsor-knotted tie.

His trip to see Wayne Bell routed him through downtown.
People jammed the streets on their way to work. Passing between
skyscrapers, he was struck that thousands of people worked in these
steel and glass enclosures.

How many were happy?

How many had fulfilling work ... or lives?

How many were living paycheck to paycheck in hopes of some
fanciful future life called retirement?

How many were actually living their dream or even had a
dream?

How many had a piece of their soul die every day they entered
those buildings?

How many knew they had options that could make a
difference?

How many had their work life and life's work aligned and
integrated?

He thought it would make a fascinating study to survey all the people in one building for the answers to these questions.

Heading his car onto the interstate, he wondered about his friends. These are successful people, from all outward appearances, yet few expressed real joy in their lives. Life was rigorous rather than victorious. They seem resigned to a numbing daily grind in a legacy of complacency. He related well. Only now he had a new awareness, a sense of possibilities and hope. Perhaps John Harold had a point.

The Professor said Wayne Bell operated a business from his home. Guiding his car off the Bethel Street exit, the man followed the directions to Lindermer Avenue, where Wayne lived. He stopped at the first two-story home on the right and checked the street numbers: 4-9-7-8. This was it. After parking his car on the street, he walked to the front porch and rang the doorbell.

Wayne Bell opened the door and shook the man's hand. "Welcome! C'mon in. We have a few minutes before we leave. Let me show you around." Wayne was a tall, conditioned man with a large, easy smile, firm handshake, and engaging blue eyes. The home was spacious and well decorated. This was an affluent section of town, and Wayne's home tastefully reflected financial success.

"Thanks," said the man. He wasn't sure what to expect. Whatever could he have to discuss with a guy with a home business? It seemed incongruent to be there. Then again, Pam Dimes had taught him plenty.

The man asked, "We're leaving soon? Where are we going?"

"You'll find out," Wayne said with a laugh and a wink. "Don't worry. C'mon, let me show you my office."

The two men stepped into a good-sized room with a magnificent view of the distant mountains ablaze with autumn colors. Wayne's office was loaded with electronic gadgets and books. "I'm state of the art here with a productive environment that is highly automated. As Barbara Hemphill taught me, I'm almost paperless." Sweeping his hand toward a wall-sized set of bookcases Wayne continued his tour, "And my books — here's where I choose to be both digital and with paper. I love reading. Learning is earning. I have books on personal development, business, parenting, gardening, philosophy, biographies, and other topics. Fifteen minutes a day keeps my mind from running astray."

"I like that," said the man with an insightful chuckle.

"Pull up a chair," Wayne rolled a high-backed chair directly in front of the man. "I imagine you're wondering what you can learn from a guy running a business from his home?"

"As a matter of fact, driving over here that's exactly what I was thinking. I admit, however, I've learned more from a 'gardener' than I imagined possible. Why not a guy who works from his house?"

Wayne continued, "You're looking at the future. What you see in this office is what is happening with a huge percentage of the working population."

"To work alone at home?" asked the man.

"No. Don't confuse location with team size. I'm far from alone in my business. I have associates throughout the world. We're connected and in constant cooperation. I'm free to do what I do best more profitably. See the substance of this, not just the small format.

"One person businesses reflect the coming economic era of the solo owner in the Age of Purpose. Those of us in these businesses are economic pioneers. We're forging new ways of doing business, of relating and collaborating. The on-purpose business approach is the way of the solo owner."

The man said, "So …?"

"So there's work to be done. Does it matter whether my desk is at home or in an office or on my phone? Thanks to technology, the ways of doing business have changed forever. Our minds, bodies, and spirits are more liberated from physical locations and we're freer to do business differently and better."

"Are you proposing that each person is actually an on-purpose business?"

"Yes, absolutely."

"But what of organizations as we know them today? If we've reduced all service and production to the level of one person, don't we need some organizing factor?"

"Exactly!" Wayne exclaimed.

"Exactly what?"

Wayne was excited. "All service and production always was at the level of one person. And an organizing factor was always needed. Nothing has changed ... except who commands the organizing. That's what On-Purpose does. It enables a solo owner of one or a company with thousands to share a common structure and method of operation. If a business exists to serve, then the Four Pillars are the four corners needed to successfully scale and sustain a business of any size."

The man observed, "So the Four Pillars stand true regardless of the size of an organization."

Wayne nodded his yes.

"A solo owner? Tell me more about them," the man requested.

"A solo owner is as its name implies—a business of one person. Who are we? We're salespeople, coaches, consultants, and professionals. Some of us are individual distributors in direct-sales companies. Others are tradesmen, artists, and cottage industrialists. We're entrepreneurs. We're salaried employees who *Think Inc!* in the context of employment with one client. Every working person is a solo owner whether he or she gets it or not.

"What are we? We're a fast and flexible work force technologically networked. We fiercely guard our independence yet cherish collaboration. We're pioneers on the new frontiers of business and the economy. This work style brings us greater personal fulfillment, integration, and relationships. We are on-purpose."

The man folded his arms across his chest with skepticism. "Sounds to me like a bunch of escapists from corporate America who couldn't get a job and have this idealistic notion as unemployables."

Wayne didn't flinch. "On the contrary, we're ultimate realists. We don't seek traditional employment. We seek greater expression of our purpose, a better-led life, a sense of belonging, and the means to contribute from our strengths. We embrace the challenges of our times to enrich our lives. Growth and learning are our accepted way of life; only our personal purpose remains our constant."

The man pushed. "What of companies like mine? Do you predict the demise of large corporations?"

"No, they're moving our way. Outsourcing is just one of many clues. Many solo owners persons are part of the team that's on call as needed. Many are independent contractors being full-time on-purpose business persons who are doing more of what they do best more profitably. Some of us are forming cooperatives to gain scale, diversification, support, branding, learning, and community.

"This wave of the future," Wayne appraised, "is the ultimate on-purpose business in the smallest sense of the word. On-purpose business persons fluidly move from project to project, even job to job — not from necessity or weakness, but from choice and strength."

"Wow! I get it!" exclaimed the man.

"The Four Pillars are really universal principles guiding organizational development. It is a new approach to building and engaging teams to meaningful work and productive results."

The man motioned to the skies with his hand. "This solo owner concept seems way out there. I guess in the virtual workplace we will need a protocol for fast connection and alignment."

Wayne said, "Exactly! The way of the on-purpose business person provides a standard 'operating system,' if you will for relating, even if we're not formally related."

A bell chimed and then Eric's voice was heard emanating from his phone. "Reminder: You have an On-Purpose Peers Meeting in thirty minutes."

"Thank you," Wayne said to his phone. "Turn off reminder." He turned to the man and explained, "More technology to help me stay on-purpose and on time.

"Let's go," Wayne moved them along again into his garage. There they hopped into his car and were off to their scheduled meeting.

21
On-Purpose Peers

▼

It's simple.... We either get used to thinking about the subtle
process
of learning and sharing knowledge in dispersed, transient networks,
or we perish.

Tom Peters
The Tom Peters Seminar

Wayne pulled onto the interstate. Peering out the window into the distance, the man contemplated all that was happening. He couldn't help thinking about Fred Taylor. Had Fred seen him gallivanting about town like this, *he* would be dead instead of Fred. The Old Man measured one's commitment to the company by the time logged at the office. Over the past few months it was as if the man were participating in a personal and organizational scavenger hunt. Fred's memory and manner continued to haunt him despite all he had learned, taught, and experienced.

He thought about Wayne. *This guy is dynamic.* Remembering his proposed study of the downtown office workers, he decided to start the study informally with Wayne. If nothing else, it would make for interesting conversation.

Rather directly, he asked, "Are you happy?"

"Positively! I'm on-purpose!" Wayne replied.

"So, what's your purpose?" asked the man.

"'Radiating Joy.' My purpose statement is, 'I exist to serve by Radiating Joy.'"

"Well, you certainly are good at that. You're one of the most joyful persons I've ever met."

"Thank you. I wasn't always this way. We TOP Performers encourage each other because most people don't know what to make of us. We're going to this meeting so we can learn and share with other business persons who use the On-Purpose approach."

"Really? There are more people like you?"

Wayne smiled. "Lots more. Even in my solo business, I face the very same issues you do as president of that monolithic dinosaur you run. The differences between our two companies are tradition, formality, and control."

The "dinosaur" comments didn't sit well with him so he counter-punched, " . . . and sales."

Wayne grinned at the man's subtle attempt at the mine-is-bigger-than-yours gamesmanship. He decided to teach the man a lesson, "What kind of sales numbers do you think I do from my house?"

Regretting his childish response, the man guessed way high. "Two million dollars a year."

"Higher," Wayne coached.

The man dug his hole deeper. This time he would really overshoot the sales figure by being absurd. "Five million dollars a year."

"Higher," Wayne laughed.

"No way!" sneered the man.

"Way!" Wayne smiled unflinchingly.

The man realized Wayne was truthful. He doubled his guess. "Ten million."

"Higher" was Eric's now familiar chant.

"Twenty million dollars."

"Higher," Wayne encouraged. He was clearly enjoying this little game the man had started, and he was finishing. Finally he lowered the boom. "I'll do fifty-five million dollars this year from that home office. By the way, I'll net more profits than your company. I've read your quarterly projections; it's been a tough year. In fact, I gave more money to charities through my foundation than your company made last year."

The man was visibly shaken. "That's impossible," he stammered. "How can you operate a business of that size from one room?"

"By applying the Four Pillars of the on-purpose business with others who are doing the same."

"Where are your people?"

"They're all over. My 'little business' is really a macro-business. I have thousands of on-purpose 'partners' working with me in a variety of functions. We collaborate using the Four Pillars plus a shared infrastructure and common culture so we can gain the scale and efficiencies I mentioned earlier. That's how I've built a fifty-five-million-dollar company with a payroll of one. Even my administrative assistant is her own business. Pretty incredible, isn't it?"

"I'll say. Where did you ever come up with these ideas?" asked the man.

"My On-Purpose Peers."

"The peer learning group that Bob Scott and Frances Attwood referenced?" asked the man.

"Yes. Napoleon Hill, in his classic book *Think and Grow Rich*, wrote of the importance of a mastermind group. Hill's book was released in 1937. It offered tremendous insights and many valuable principles. Yet, Hill was a product of the Industrial Age, and much of his writing springs from that passing era. His writing was about the mind.

"We're centered on the heart. Think of it as a 'master heart' group. We call them On-Purpose Peers Meetings."

The On-Purpose Peers

It was one revelation after the next. Wayne pulled the car into a parking space next to a suburban hotel. They entered the lobby. Wayne led the man to a boardroom.

There was a tap on the man's shoulder, and a familiar voice said, "Welcome, friend." The man was surprised that it was Perry James, accompanied by Bob Scott. They warmly greeted him.

Perry said, "I'm happy you're here today. Many years ago Hal Trudy founded this On-Purpose Peers Meeting. Some begin the process, few commit to it, and fewer still are considered for membership. Others, like your old boss Fred Taylor, never took an interest in having a peer group.

"We have one rule here: Anything you hear in this room is confidential. Agreed?"

"Agreed," said the man. He was flattered to be included.

Bob graciously introduced the man to each on-purpose business person in the room. He recognized many of them as prominent people in the community.

The man asked, "Is the Professor here?"

Bob answered, "No, he participates in one for educators. There are meetings for different spheres of influence."

"How many meetings for different professions are there?" the man probed.

"Many. There are Peers Meetings for nonprofit organizations, government, arts and entertainment, sports, churches, and others."

"Do the groups ever meet jointly?"

"Occasionally," Bob replied. "Those are more like conferences. Everyone is welcome. They're fun. The rich diversity is impressive. Let's talk later—Perry is about to start the meeting."

They sat around the conference table. Each person gave an update on a variety of personal and work matters. As one spoke, the others made notes in journals.

The Pillars came alive before the man's eyes. For the next few hours, this board of mutual advisors intensively analyzed, critiqued, focused, and developed one another's personal and professional lives and businesses with a rare insight and accountability. Everything was open for discussion.

They dealt with strategic issues, then brainstormed projects, problems, and opportunities. Sometimes they networked to connect each other with resources. Each person had ample time to voice his or her needs. Laughter frequently filled the room in this hardworking and congenial group.

When the Peers Meeting ended, Wayne had to run to another meeting. Bob Scott gave the man a ride to Wayne's house to pick up his car. He inquired, "What did you think of our time together?"

"I was blown away," the man bubbled. "I've never experienced anything like that before. The collective advice, wisdom, and creativity generated energy unlike any I've ever felt. It was as if an invisible presence were guiding the meeting."

"That Tingle is the presence and power of being on-purpose. You experienced pure service in a community of on-purpose business persons who are leading on-purpose businesses."

Bob continued, "We just had two openings in our Peers Meeting. We're extending you an invitation to join us. We've been cultivating you for some time and feel you're ready. Are you interested?"

The man jumped at the opportunity. "Yes, count me in. I'm honored. How in the world do you have two openings? Who in their right mind would leave a group like that?"

Bob grinned. "We're having a 'baby.' Two members of our group birthed a new one. Their departure is a sign of healthy growth. They've been trained to facilitate the meetings. It's special when we reproduce like cells. It means that more people go deeper in their on-purpose journey.

"By the way, the other person who will soon be invited to join is Pam Dimes."

"That's great," said the man, beaming. "Tell me the details." Bob Scott proceeded to spell out the guidelines and commitments for participation. The ride was a blur for the man. His head spun with excitement.

22
The Interview

▼

For what shall it profit a man, if he shall gain the whole world, and lose his own soul?

Jesus Christ
Mark 9:36 (KJV)

The reporter sat with her pen and paper, furiously scribbling notes. The interview had lasted more than two hours. Yet for the man and the reporter, it seemed only minutes since she had asked her opening question.

Finally she placed her pen on her pad and said, "Remarkable. Do you continue your On-Purpose Peers Meetings?"

"Faithfully. I rarely miss. Some members who've moved away fly back to attend. Others join a meeting in their new hometown or start their own."

"This is incredible. How many of these groups exist?"

"Lots. I honestly don't know the number. They happen through the On-Purpose Planet."

"Next question: What happened with the GEOMay contract?"

"We kept the contract. It's been better than any of us imagined. We've even formed a joint venture with GEOMay Company. We've raised our standards to new levels of TOP performance, thanks to that relationship."

"There are just two more questions that remain unanswered, then we can wrap up this interview." Checking the hour from the gold pocket watch on the man's desk, she added, "We've been at this awhile."

"Ask me your question," the man invited.

She flipped through her notebook. "I want to go back to something. Why are you going public about all this?"

"That's simple. I promised the Professor and Bob that I would share what I learned about being on-purpose. I'm not 'going public,' to use your term. I'm simply answering your questions. Perhaps you're the first reporter to pick up on it as newsworthy."

She said, "I must admit, there's a bigger story here than I anticipated."

The Gold Watch

"And your last question?" he asked.

"The gold watch. Tell me the story of this gold watch."

"Ah, the gold watch," he reflected. "That's what brings all this together. The week after my visit to the Peers Meeting, Mrs. Taylor came by my office. She gave me Fred's gold pocket watch from his retirement party and a personal note penned by him. The watch reminds me of Fred's message. Fred's note was the clarion call that radically shifted my personal perspective, and ultimately the course of this business. Ironically, perhaps Fred's greatest contribution to this company was made after his death."

"How?" urged the reporter.

"When Mrs. Taylor came to see me she said, 'My late husband was fond of you. You probably realized it, yet rarely heard it. Fred was a stoic man whose ways were ... shall I say, set in concrete. It was his strength; yet in the end it proved to be his Achilles' heel. Holding in his feelings contributed to his stress and heart disease, which ultimately led to his premature death.'

"I said, 'Yes, ma'am, I know Fred cared a great deal about his work, this company, and its people. He didn't openly express it much. His actions spoke loudly, even if he didn't.'

"She thanked me with a warm smile and continued, 'He sacrificed much for the business. Those of us closest to him also paid a high price. His heart problems forced him to face death. Fred was a thorough man. He prepared for his death. He wanted to reach out to those of you with whom he worked.

"'With his remaining time he sought to make amends. Within our family, many hurts were healed. While he struggled to express himself verbally, he became quite eloquent and free with a pen in hand.'

"I nodded in respect and didn't utter a word. Her eyes teared up, and her voice wavered. She then said, 'We had a good marriage. Fred confided many things to me. Feelings frightened him. He feared not being needed, not being a good leader. He feared change and many other ghosts. As the monthly financial statements went, so did Fred's emotions.

"'He had nowhere and no one to turn to in these times. The complexity of his business problems was beyond my experience and advice. I often wondered how he held up under the pressure. His job was everything to him — it was his identity.'

"'Yes, Mrs. Taylor,' I said. 'Fred was dedicated to this company.' I wasn't sure where she was leading, so I continued listening.

"'Dedicated! To a fault!' Mrs. Taylor scolded. Now more animated, she resumed, 'Did you know these last years as CEO were his worst years? After all those years of climbing the corporate ladder of success, finally reaching the highest rung — and all he found was loneliness, confusion, and frustration. The rapid changes in the marketplace and the demise of the old ways of doing business all contributed to his quiet depression in the midst of external "success."

"'His inability to reach out forced him to go somewhere. He turned inward, in a most negative way. All his emotions shut down except gut-wrenching frustration. Knowing that he was responsible for the erosion of the company's market leadership was his most devastating realization. It weighed heavily on him. His instincts, honed over forty-eight years, which had served him so well, were now betraying him.

"'The world changed, but Fred clung to the past. As the company spiraled downward, so did Fred's emotional and physical health. He was caught in a web of his own making. His options were played.'

"I said, 'I had no idea Fred was going through so much. If only he had asked for help, certainly ...'

"'If only!' she abruptly interrupted. 'If only. Oh, how I hate those two little words. In Fred's last days we talked about our life together, our children's lives, and his life and career. Fred kept saying, "If only I had known about this or that." My husband came to view his whole life against those two words, "If only..." With death looming near, he summoned his remaining strength and decided no more "if onlys."'

"I said, 'I'm not sure I understand.'

"'Fred was determined,' she continued, 'to bring positive closure on a life filled with regrets and "if onlys." That's my reason for seeing you. You are one of the people he wanted to reach. I am Fred's messenger. His hope is that you'll learn from his life.'"

The reporter said, "This is pretty heavy. What happened next?"

The man resumed, "And what a messenger Mrs. Taylor was. Her face, words, presence, posture, and conviction were almost angelic. It was as if God was speaking through her to me."

The Gift

"Mrs. Taylor continued, 'May I present my late husband's gift and message for you?'

"She handed me a small, neatly wrapped box and a letter with my name, hand-addressed. I recognized Fred's handwriting.

"Opening the package, I found Fred's retirement pocket watch. I thought it was a nice gesture. I pried open the soft gold cover with my thumbnail and read the inscription, 'To Frederick W. Taylor, in honor of forty-eight years of faithful service and leadership.' I was touched that Fred bequeathed his prized watch to me. I understood it to represent his life's work.

"Little did I know what was in store for me in Fred's letter. I read it aloud."

The man opened his desk drawer, pulled out a folder, and began to read to the reporter:

To my friend and business associate,

My days are numbered and my words to you long past due. Even as my physical strength drains, I find a renewed strength and faith in a peace that passes all understanding.

Reflecting on my life, I come to this final passage called death. In the end it is my loving wife and children who are with me. I've sought forgiveness from many and especially them.

It was my damn unavailability. I was so busy building a business that I forgot to build a life. I was too busy for ball games, recitals, birthdays, and just plain hanging around with my family. I realize it isn't as simple as quality time. The key is available time. If I'm not raising my children, then someone else is. Thank goodness for my wife — at least they had one of us. My kids missed out on having a father, and my wife on a husband.

I was a provider, but not a parent or husband. Make no mistake; a father and husband were preferred to a provider. I remain proud of my lifetime of business accomplishments; yet, today they are but hollow achievements from my new vantage point.

It's ironic that a neglected heart is killing me and yet setting me free to be me. Clinically it's called coronary disease. Realistically, it is my dis-ease with life itself — the emptiness inside my heart nearly cost me my wife, my family, the business, and, ultimately, is claiming my life.

Had I exercised my heart physically and emotionally, perhaps I, too, could have had an active and long retirement like a man I know named Hal Trudy. Get to know him. He'll share truth with you which years ago I regrettably rejected as hogwash. I was too skeptical and arrogant to learn. Hal was right! Hal is finishing strong and well.

The man smiled. "Isn't it amazing! I probably met Hal about the time Fred was composing this letter. He probably had no idea Hal and I were meeting." He returned to reading Fred's letter.

So a physical and emotional hardness of heart is the culprit of my condition. What were my options? How might I have done it all differently? If only I had built my life from the inside out instead of from the outside in, I know beyond any reasonable doubt that the health and well-being of my family, the company, and I would be more richly blessed. I leave a legacy of transactions, not one of a company.

I accept responsibility for my ill-fated decisions. My choices led me to this irreversible point of physical decline. My destiny is determined; only the date remains unknown. You are no different than I, except you have more options. You have choices that have not been fully played out to their ultimate conclusion.

That's why I'm bequeathing you my pocket watch. I want it to serve as a constant reminder to learn from my errors before the eleventh hour of your life.

You, like me, are consumed with your career and the success of the business, which are definitely honorable aspirations in the proper perspective. As the Ghost of Christmas Future did for Ebenezer Scrooge in Charles Dickens' *A Christmas Carol*, I hope I, too, am lifting the veil to your future. My path was a dead end. If only you knew what I know now, you would live your life and do business differently. You would find your way home.

Our personal lives are more important than our professional lives. Is that a startling revelation? For me it was! I measured my life by what I did, what I earned, and what job I had. Please don't misunderstand me. Work and a career are honorably important. After all, God put Adam on the earth to work the garden, not to be on some feel-good vacation seven days a week.

The man smiled and commented, "That's vintage Fred." Continuing the letter, he read,

Even Adam in the Garden of Eden needed companionship in addition to God. Sharing life — this is the real wealth of living.

Look at the long-term price of my misplaced priorities. How many men and women of high competence and quality of character did I drive from our company? How many did I burn out in the name of quarterly results? It was a short-term, high-payoff strategy with long-run destructive implications. I failed to offer meaningful work and to foster a sense of community.

You, on the other hand, have a chance to change it. You set the environment as the leader. Don't idly agree that our personal lives are more important than our professional lives; embrace this truth. People watch your actions. Lead by example. Instill this value in the company.

Create a business where personal and professional lives can exist in harmony. Create a community where the business supports the person and family instead of the person and family supporting the business. With my way, the price is too dear. It wasn't even good business.

Great companies come from great people. Great companies cannot make great people. We as leaders play a key role in helping ordinary people accomplish extraordinary results. The rewards accrue to all. We can never rise above the collective personal greatness of the people around us. Work must be more than a paycheck. Tap into the "more," and you tap into people's genius.

It begins with you — the leader of the company. Get straight personally. It's the best thing you can do for the business.

Yes, my gold pocket watch is to be a reminder of my way of life and my career successes and my failures. I nearly blew it all! Belatedly, I've been graced with a little time in the waning days of my life to salvage a remnant. I'm taking action now. I don't ever recall being so alive. Ironically, in the midst of dying, death is setting me free. I'm expressing my love to my wife, children, and grandchildren as never before. No more "if onlys." The past is the past. No future regrets. No future regrets!

You are my hope and my professional legacy. You can alter the course of events. You can redeem my regrets if you accept my challenge. It begins with you and now it rests with you. Listen to a man with a whole life perspective. Yes, the business matters. No, it is not the source of our true identity and success. At best, it is a place to live out and express a portion of our purpose in life.

I beseech you to take up this message and turn to a new manner of conducting yourself and the company.

Sincerely yours,

Frederick W. Taylor

The man paused for a long moment, then looked straight at the reporter as he continued his reverie. "Tears welled in my eyes. Mrs. Taylor became a watery blur as Fred's message sank into my being. I said to Mrs. Taylor, 'I'm speechless as to why Fred would reach out to me like this.'

"'That's easy, because the two of you are so alike,' she told me.

"'We are not!' I protested.

"'Oh, yes, you are. Why do you think you became Fred's replacement? The board knew the company was built around a hard-driving skeptic who was committed to little else but his career and this company. They replaced Fred with another Fred. Fred told me so himself.

"'You were the only one who fit the job description. The Old Man, yes I knew that was his nickname, said, "He's the man. You can't teach him a thing unless you whack him over the head with a stick. When I was his age I was the same way, and look at where it got me."'

"'I didn't know I was like Fred,' I said.

"'How could you not know?' she replied in disbelief."

The man turned again to the reporter. "Can you believe it? I didn't know that I didn't know. Fred possessed every quality I despised—in myself. It was no wonder I couldn't get him out of my thoughts. We were so much alike. Fred was my mentor whether I realized it or not.

"Rarely does one get to glimpse into a crystal ball. Fred lifted the curtain to the future, and I didn't like what I saw. Some changes in my life were long overdue. The Four Pillars showed me a different path than the one Fred and I had been traveling. All I learned about the on-purpose business was meaningless, unless I accepted Fred's challenge.

"My spirit was torn and my heart was touched. This was my epiphany, my wake-up call for life that solidified all I had been learning. I looked up from Fred's note and said, 'Mrs. Taylor, Fred was a good man. I wouldn't be where I am today had he not cared about me. I accept his challenge to live life differently here at work — and at home.'

"Her face brightened with a smile. She rose and approached me. I respectfully rose from my chair. Gently placing a hand on each side of my face, she gazed at me as if I were a newborn. In fact, I felt like one who had been washed clean. I had been given a new lease on life. No 'if onlys.' She pulled my face toward hers and tenderly kissed me on my cheek as if to seal the conviction of my commitment.

"Mrs. Taylor's closing remarks to me were 'Fred was a good man. You now know the man I married and the man I buried. In between, my husband lost himself. In the eleventh hour, he finally found himself and his way home. Thank you for answering his lament. God bless you!'

"And with that, she turned and walked out the door."

The reporter sat hushed and wide-eyed. "What did you do next?"

"I sat alone at my desk holding Fred's gold pocket watch and letter. I was dumbfounded. I cradled the pocket watch in my hand for the longest time. I don't know how long I sat there just staring at it and thinking. Finally, I picked up the phone and dialed.

"'Hello,' came my wife's voice.

"I said, 'Hi, honey! I'm coming home early tonight. I want to share a gift for us that Mrs. Taylor brought by from Fred. I've learned some things here at work that will help us. Let's talk about making our lives and marriage on-purpose.'

"'Are you all right?' my wife asked.

"'I'm fine,' I said. 'Also, I'm making an appointment to see a man named John Harold. He has something I need. Go with me. It is something you've wanted for us for a long time. Now I do, too. Sorry, honey, I didn't know what you know.'

"'Are you sure you're okay?' she double-checked.

"'Sweetie, I've never been better,' I assured her. '"I love you and I'm coming home.'"

Acknowledgments
To the Original 1998 Edition

It always amazes me to watch the movie credits roll and see all the people involved in making it. Similarly, I'm stunned reflecting on all the people who have left their imprint on this work. I'm humbled to realize so many people cared enough to give of themselves.

First, I must thank my family. My children, Charles and Anne, have watched me disappear into my home office for hours on end. I asked them not to disturb me. And as two kids under age seven, they honored my request almost as many times as they didn't. Oh, well! What delightful interruptions. My wife, Judith, helped make time for my writing by managing schedules to accommodate those truly intense, yet flowing times of work. My parents and my brother, Bob, are loving and generous champions with my family and work. Without them, none of this would be possible. My mother-in-law, AKA Granny, opened Woodlawn for long family respites that provided extended and uninterrupted writing opportunities while I stayed home.

For his always forthright opinions and editing on the original manuscript, I hold Paul Crowell in highest esteem. What an example of a servant-friend! Paul, I'm passing along your example to others. Randy Robertson, Alan Skelton, Glenn Hettinger, Gary Hatter, and Kirk Squires all gave detailed and honest feedback on the first (and more lengthy) manuscripts.

My clients have willingly provided an open acceptance for my on-purpose perspective. I'm especially appreciative of George Maynard and his team at Orlando Regional Healthcare Foundation. Having a client in my hometown committed to making this dream a reality has been a blessing. More importantly, I value the friendship. To Susan Batchelor who ten years ago engaged me to teach an hour and a half presentation to a group of real estate brokers on strategic planning . . . little did we know what was begun.

Others of special note are: Steve Levee, Bruce Nygren, Murray Fisher, Bert Ghezzi, Jim Keeter, Mark Modesti, Greg Voisen, Jeff Tallman, Jay Brophy, my professors at The Darden School, the professors and mentors of The On-Purpose College, Mark Eldridge, Elsom Eldridge, Jr., Pam Dean, Karen Nichols, Marilu Hall, Monica Calzolari, Claire Carter, Chic Thompson, Dana Kyle, Laurie Hartman, Lisa Williams, Mark Kellum, Perry Nies, Hal and Trudy Williamson, Robert and Jamie Thomas, Jackie Wildermann, Tom Farr, Paul Chiampa, Charlie Stuart, John Smith, Don Curran, Dr. George Andreae, Faye Hobbs, Gordon Caswell, Terry Taylor, the team at Bob Smith's American ReproGraphics and especially Peggy, Hank Franklin, Joe Barnes, and John Rosenblum. Each in his or her own special way either opened doors for me or tried to kick me through one when I needed it.

Thank you to the men and women who wrote endorsements. You are kind to place the mantle of your good name and reputation upon this book. I especially want to thank Mark Victor Hansen for his foreword.

Many readers of *The On-Purpose Person* have called or written the office asking for *The On-Purpose Business*. These almost daily phone calls have been a true source of encouragement. Thank you.

Thank you to the publishing team at Piñon Press and NavPress. Dean Galiano is directly responsible for this book being where it belongs. Thanks, Dean, for your steadfast belief in the importance of being on-purpose. Thanks, Kent Wilson, for being open and willing for NavPress to be a publishing partner in this endeavor. Sue Geiman and Nanci McAllister fostered me through the transitions with skill and warmth. Lori Mitchell was the managing editor who skillfully managed this manuscript and even more skillfully managed me! The others in editing, design, sales and marketing, PR and operations—Thanks! I'm proud to be a small part of the NavPress and Navigator family.

Please forgive me if I failed to mention your name in thanks. It would only be an oversight, not ... on-purpose.

Last but not least, I thank God for this awesome gift and message of being on-purpose. I am finally willing to be a faithful steward and bold professor of this message. When I am at my eleventh hour, I hope and pray that I soon will hear you say, "Well done, good and faithful servant; you have been faithful over a little, I will set you over much; enter into the joy of your Master."

About the Author

Kevin McCarthy first read the book *I'm OK, You're OK*, in 1968. This was the start of a personal development process that took him through thousands of hours of reading, contemplating, searching, listening, and discovering. It culminated in *The On-Purpose Person*, his first book. Kevin is a classically educated businessman with a strong entrepreneurial inclination. He graduated from Lehigh University with a Bachelor of Science degree in business and economics. After three years in corporate banking and general management of a small business, graduate business school was the logical next step. Kevin received his MBA from The Darden School of the University of Virginia in 1982.

Kevin founded US Partners, Inc., dba On-Purpose Partners in 1983. He offered his first On-Purpose Business workshop for real estate brokers in 1989. This strategic planning approach was geared to those who needed to plan strategically, yet lacked the time, experience, or inclination. The method was simple: "Love your work, know why, and here's how." That seminar became the basis for *The On-Purpose Business Person*.

Kevin was born on Christmas Day in Pittsburgh, PA. He graduated from Shady Side Academy. Today, he lives in the Orlando, FL area with his wife, Judith, and children Charles and Anne. He's active in his church and community. He reads biographies, business, and personal development books.

"I'm the steward of a gift called 'being on-purpose.' I'm in awe seeing this message profoundly touching lives and influencing organizations. It's a privilege I'm compelled to share."

He is a Professional Member of the National Speakers Association and offers webcasts, keynote addresses, workshops, and seminars about being on-purpose.

Resources

Do you want your business or career to be on-purpose?

On-Purpose® can help. We have business advisors and coaches who are experienced practitioners with diverse backgrounds and common beliefs in the value of being on-purpose.

Please visit our websites to find the many resources available to help you.

- www.on-purpose.com — the gateway to all things on-purpose and bookstore
- www.on-purposeba.com — site for On-Purpose Business Advisors
- www.kevinwmccarthy.com — Kevin's personal and business leadership video blog

We're dedicated to your development and growth as an on-purpose person and business person.

Our Online Bookstore offers various on-purpose resources such as books, workbooks, audios, and other items to enhance your efforts to be on-purpose.

ON PURPOSE®

P.O. Box 1568
Winter Park, FL 32790-1568
(407) 657-6000

www.on-purpose.com

Made in the USA
Charleston, SC
15 June 2015